UNHOLY PLEASURE

For Derwent May

UNHOLY PLEASURE

OR

THE IDEA OF
SOCIAL CLASS

*

P. N. FURBANK

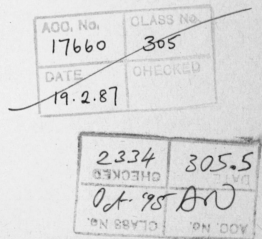
OXFORD UNIVERSITY PRESS

1986

Oxford University Press, Walton Street, Oxford OX2 6DP

Oxford New York Toronto
Delhi Bombay Calcutta Madras Karachi
Petaling Jaya Singapore Hong Kong Tokyo
Nairobi Dar es Salaam Cape Town
Melbourne Auckland

and associated companies in
Beirut Berlin Ibadan Nicosia

Oxford is a trade mark of Oxford University Press

First published 1985
First issued as an Oxford University Press paperback 1986

British Library Cataloguing in Publication Data
Furbank, P. N.
Unholy pleasure, or, The idea of social
class.
1. Social classes.
I. Title
305.5   HT609
ISBN 0–19–285147–0

Printed in Great Britain

CONTENTS

ACKNOWLEDGEMENTS

My warmest thanks are due to the following, who read drafts of portions of this book and made criticisms: Andrew Best, John Bossy, Piers Brendon, Roger Day, Simon Eliot, Virginia Llewellyn Smith, Graham Martin, Arthur Marwick, Derwent May, Bob Owens; also to Lorna Hardwick, Jim Milroy, and Peter Rickard for advice; to Douglas Matthews, who compiled the Index; and to Pat Wallace, who typed the manuscript.

NOTE

Translations from the French are my own, except where otherwise indicated.

PART 1

*

THE MEANING OF 'CLASS'

'It sometimes appears [said Mr Touchett] as if the young women in the lower class were not very well treated; but I guess their position is better in the upper and even to some extent in the middle.'

'Gracious,' Isabel exclaimed; 'how many classes have they? About fifty, I suppose.'

'Well, I don't know that I ever counted them. I never took much notice of the classes. That's the advantage of being an American here; you don't belong to any class.'

'I hope so,' said Isabel. 'Imagine one's belonging to an English class!'

(Henry James, *The Portrait of a Lady*)

1

The rhetoric of 'class'

People in Britain at the moment talk much too much about 'class'. Some taboo was broken in the 1950s, round about the time of Richard Hoggart's *The Uses of Literacy*, and since then everyone has felt a freedom and a compulsion to use 'class language'. It is done with a sort of tacit defiance of the Edwardian 'good form' convention that 'decent people know these things but don't talk about them'. And it should be a good thing; but in practice, to tell the truth, the chatter grows slightly odious.

It also grows bewildering. Take the phrase 'middle class'. When people use it, you have no hope of guessing what they mean without many questions about *them*—who they are, whom they are talking to, and with what end in view. One thing, indeed, may safely be assumed, that what is intended is a sneer; and if you probe, what you are hoping to find is still not a definition—what does the speaker mean by 'middle class'?—so much as a purpose or set of purposes—what is the speaker up to? These purposes are more often than not aggressive. I will give an example, a skirmish fought with cunning and resourcefulness on both sides, from a radio interview with Lady Longford in 1979.

INTERVIEWER (*in a tone of bluff innocence*): Would it be right to say you come from a comfortable middle-class family?

LADY LONGFORD (*in astonishment*): *Upper* middle class. (*Then, realizing the trap laid for her, continues hastily*) . . . That was what we were told. I never knew what it meant. I investigated later, but I could never find out. It doesn't exist.

This is the sort of issue that the word 'class' conjures up for many people, together with lore about 'class' shibboleths ('Lord Beauchamp thought it middle class not to decant champagne') and the detective-work that goes with shibboleths. Later in my book I shall try to suggest how and why, round about the 1830s, the 'class-shibboleth' idea became important in England and certain shibboleths—archetypically the 'dropped *h*'—were institutionalized. (It is a curious and complex story.) Here, rather, what I am concerned

with is the mock-sociological game of spotting, and gleefully rival-
ling others in spotting, hidden 'social indicators'. John Betjeman,
who capitalized on it himself, evoked it thus:

> A single topic occupies our minds.
> 'Tis hinted at or boldly blazoned in
> Our accents, clothes and ways of eating fish,
> And being introduced and taking leave,
> 'Farewell', 'So long', 'Bunghosky', 'Cheeribye'—
> That topic all-absorbing, as it was,
> Is now and ever shall be, to us—CLASS.[1]

It is held to be amusing, when played as a parlour-game by Jilly
Cooper or in the *Official Sloane Ranger Handbook*; but the game pretty
soon becomes malodorous. I hardly need stress that what is involved
is not a form of sociology, even of amateur sociology, but rather a
form of competitive social behaviour of the very kind it pretends to
be studying. It is always, and of necessity, a sort of 'wallowing', to be
enjoyed with 'unholy pleasure'.

Indeed I am tempted to rail and denounce it, like some Carlyle.
But then I look into my own breast and find . . . Well, what do I
find? A strange assortment of things actually: a readiness to be dis-
honest on the subject of 'class', and some quite cunning techniques
for this purpose; and then again a mass of ideas on 'class', acquired
mainly in childhood, some of which are plainly the foolishest folk-
lore, but of which others seem as if they might be fragments of a
coherent theory, or perhaps of several distinct and coherent theories.
During any day, encounters with people induce in me what Arthur
Marwick has called 'images of class',[2] which seem to imply a 'class-
system', but like all mental images they are evanescent and will not
bear much scrutiny. Then in a separate compartment of my breast I
find ideas drawn from books by historians and sociologists, and
especially a number from Marx.

Without doubt there is a lot of stuff there, and it seems to be part
of my being; but it is in a state of disorder, and if I find the subject
odious this may partly be the reason, i.e. irritation with myself for
not better organizing my mental life. For instance, are those 'coherent theories' that I seem to glimpse a reality, and can they be spelled
out, and can it be discovered where and when they were devised?
Again, *ought* I to allow my thoughts on 'class' to be separated into
compartments? One thing seems clear: if one is to study 'class', the
human breast is a very good place to study it—that is to say, it must
be done very considerably by introspection; and, what is much the

same thing, it must be done by the examination of *words*—that is to say, of the way 'class' vocabulary functions for oneself when one uses it. It is very much, from one point of view, a linguistic problem and belongs to that '*large* class of cases' in which, according to Wittgenstein, 'the meaning of a word is its use in the language'.[3]

Could it be agreed, anyway, that it is a leading characteristic of the terms 'class' and 'classes', in their social sense, that we tend to use them in something approaching conscious bad faith? In discussing people or societies there is a temptation, and we succumb to it, to call something or somebody 'middle class' or 'working class' or 'upper class' in order to sound more specific than we are actually able to be. What we are doing, really, is to leave it to our interlocutor to fill out the phrases with content. 'These are the words that people use,' we tell ourselves, 'so it must be proper to use them. And they may give to others a clear picture of some human group, some collection of human faces, even if they don't to us.'

I do not mean that we always use them in bad faith. Sometimes we employ them with a kind of confidence. We use, shall we say, the phrase 'middle-class housing', and a convincing vision flashes before our mental eye: polished doorknockers, perhaps, or windows with Staffordshire dogs in them and the *Guardian* on the doorstep. However, if we are honest with ourselves, the confidence is only momentary: press with any weight on the concept 'middle-class housing', try to follow it through as a viable sociological or architectural description, and it flies to pieces, the vision dissolves.

What this brings home to us is that the terms 'middle class', 'upper class', 'working class' work most unproblematically not as nouns but as *epithets*— impressionistic epithets. They are thus nearer to the language of ethics (which is entirely a matter of epithets) than we tend to think, and were we always to remember this when we use them they would pose less of a puzzle; but then they would also lose half of their seductiveness. For their power and attraction seem to lie, partly, precisely in the scope that they offer for prevarication, deviousness and the playing of social and political games. They are, essentially, rhetorical concepts.

By now we know a fair amount about the rise of the terms 'class' and 'classes' in their social sense. As Asa Briggs has described in his article 'The Language of "Class" in Nineteenth-century England',[4] the terms first assumed importance in England—tending to replace words like 'rank', 'order', 'degree', 'condition', 'estate'—at the beginning of the nineteenth century. This seems to have been the result, or at any rate the concomitant, of the political struggles leading up to the first Reform Act. The concepts of 'ranks' or 'orders' etc. tacitly imply a rightness and divinely appointed necessity in social inequality. (Though, by the way, we must remember not to take this talk of 'ranks' and 'orders' literally or imagine, as is sometimes quaintly done, that everyone in 'Old England' possessed an ascertainable rank.) Now, in the 1820s most even of the opponents of parliamentary reform paid some lip-service to legal equality, in however attenuated a form. Thus there was a need for a less obviously tendentious terminology for social difference; and 'class', a 'value-free' term of logic, filled the bill very neatly. Further it may be held (this is the view of Harold Perkin and others) that why this change of language took place just then is because it was at this time (not before, and also not later) that a middle class and a working class came into existence (and came into existence as a product of each other).

We must be clear, though, as to what we mean when we speak of 'class' terminology as superseding an older one. The term 'class' was already in fairly frequent use in the later eighteenth century in such phrases as 'of the lowest class', 'members of the operative class', 'the middling class'. The development we are concerned with is a more significant one, viz., that in the 1820s people started to talk in terms of a 'class'-system, composed of three classes arranged by relative position or 'height';* and equally important, that they showed themselves ready, on occasion at least, to ascribe *themselves* to a 'class'. (This latter naturally had a large influence on 'class'-naming. You might ascribe yourself to the 'working class' or 'working classes', but you would hardly be likely to dub yourself a member of 'the inferior class'. Likewise, you would be more likely to ascribe yourself to the 'middle class' than to the 'middling class'.)

The uses of ambiguity

Let us notice an ambiguity about the way in which, now as in the 1820s, we use the terms 'class' and 'classes'. We sometimes talk of the 'middle class' or the 'working class' and at other of the 'middle

---

* It is perhaps worth pointing out that a 'middle class', in this sense, is an idea conceivable only in cultures which express relative valuation in terms of height ('inferior', 'superior', etc.) It would not have been conceptually possible in ancient Greece which, if we may judge from Aristotle's *Politics*, did not employ this metaphor of height.

class*es*' or 'working class*es*'. Now it might be supposed that what is
meant by 'the middle classes' is 'all the classes within the middle
class', but this would suggest a very shaky grasp of the theory of
classification, which works in a quite different way. What is actually
meant, as a little introspection will suggest, is rather 'all the different
people composing the middle class'—a quite natural, though subtle,
English idiom, also found in the army phrase 'other ranks', meaning
actual soldiers. (A corporal is told to 'detail five other ranks to dig a
latrine'.) A speaker may have various motives for using the plural
form in this way. It may be 'I am not sure I quite like all this talk of
"the middle class" (*or* "the working class" *or* "the upper class").
After all, there are so many different sorts of people, such glorious
variety, in the middle class. Don't let us be Procrustean.' There may
again—indeed there certainly was in the Reform Bill period—a
strong political motive on the part of the Tory-minded not to use the
singular form and thereby admit the existence of a unified 'working
class'. Asa Briggs, in his article, notes that Peel would have nothing
to do with the word 'class'. (It was for similar semi-political motives
that Evangelicals were fond of addressing exhortations to the 'Upper
(or Higher) and Middle (or Middling) Classes'.)[5]

Triadic schemes

I come next to the fact that, in the English version of 'class', there
are three 'classes', upper, middle, and lower. This is the basic concept, though it is modified in all sorts of ways under the pressure of
real-life conflicts.* (And of course its tripartite pattern makes a fundamental difference between it and the Marxist or 'Continental'
scheme, which is binary, viz., bourgeois and proletariat.) It is, if one
scrutinizes it, a scheme with paradoxical characteristics. For the
word 'class' makes a powerful rhetorical gesture towards the 'scientific' and the value-free: it seems to suggest that what is involved is
something like natural-history classification. (This indeed, given the
réclame of such classification in the later eighteenth century, must
have been part of its attraction at the time of its adoption.) On the

---

* A three-class system on the railways goes back to very early days and may be
seen in Ackermann's long prints of trains in 1831. When, in 1872, Midland Railways
opted for a two-class system, they did so by dropping the second class, leaving the
name of the third unchanged—thus preserving at least the ghost of a tripartite
scheme. Their action, none the less, was decried by some as a 'Jacobinical blow at the
sanctity of caste'. (See Hamilton Ellis, *Railway Carriages in the British Isles* (1965),
p. 30.)

other hand, and from another point of view, this English 'social class' concept is purely and simply *about* evaluation—much more so even than earlier social concepts, like 'orders', 'quality', 'degree' etc. 'Class' says nothing more at all about humans than that they are higher, or in the middle, or lower.

However, whatever the word 'class' may suggest, with 'social class' we are not really concerned with *classification*, as in botany or librarianship. What we are concerned with, rather, is a scheme somewhat on the same lines as that medieval *scheme* the Three Orders or the Three Estates, the triad of Those Who Pray/Those Who Fight/Those Who Work. And what strikes one about both schemes is how well they are adapted to express whatever the speaker wants them to express.

It is fascinating to follow, in Georges Duby's history of the 'Three Orders',[6] the endless succession of ways in which it was found this scheme could be exploited. By Gérard de Cambrai and Adalbert de Laon, in the eleventh century, the scheme was made to assert that *bishops* should run society and that princes would do well to bishopize themselves; by Benoît de Sainte Maure, a century and a half later, it was made to assert that *princes* should run society, with the aid of a special relationship with knights. Again, 'Those Who Work' were identified at certain times with peasants, at others with *merchants*.

It was an absolute gift to ideology, this triad, nor did it cease to be after it was actually incarnated in the Three Estates of the French body politic. The historian Georges Dumézil,[7] indeed, argues that a certain triad of functions—Magical and juridical sovereignty/Military force/Productive 'abundance'—are a basic pattern of Indo-European and Indo-Iranian thought, to be traced not only in the 'three orders' of Gérard and Adalbert but in Scandinavian mythology, the legendary founding-stories of Rome, and the Hindu caste-system. But we need not follow him here into the *content* of tripartite notions; for our purposes, anyway, we need look no further than their *form*. Music constantly reminds us of the endless *formal* resources of the triad: you can permute the order of the notes, you can conjoin two against a third, you can play all three as a chord etc. And the supreme message of the triad is, of course, concord: two is the number of discord, three is the number of concord. Nothing could better suit the purposes of ideology. Compare *Those Who Pray/Those Who Fight/Those Who Work* with *Upper Class/Middle Class/Lower (or Working) Class*. Both have a satisfying air of completeness, and what they also declare, though the second declares it in more muted tones, is that society is a harmony—its components work inextricably together for the greater good of mankind or the glory of God.

Now these satisfying 'systems' are quite illusory and, under scrutiny, fly into a hundred fragments. (The crack is already visible in that hesitation how to name the third 'class'—'Lower'? or 'Working'?) To the innocent observer, these schemes might appear to be *classifications*, but this would be an error. *Classification* would work more as follows: 'Humans in society are (bifurcation 1) either men of prayer or not men of prayer; the latter are (bifurcation 2) military men or non-military men. Here classification ends, and it is only by a *fiat* on somebody's part that 'non-military men' is to be identified with 'workers'.

Let me give another example of a 'scheme'. In 1834 John Stuart Mill complained how social commentators would revolve in an 'eternal circle' of 'landlords, capitalists and labourers' ('until they seem to think of the distinction of society into those three classes as if it were one of God's ordinances, not man's'.)[8] Plainly the charm of that familiar scheme Landlords/Capitalists/Labourers is partly aesthetic. With its attractive triadic shape, it somehow looks or sounds as if it were exhaustive—though any such exhaustiveness is quite illusory. Where would one place shopkeepers in this scheme, or doctors, or John Stuart Mill himself? With all such schemes what one needs to keep in mind is the trickery built into their form.

The species-fallacy

I was perhaps too sweeping in denying any connection between social 'class' and classification. For in the way some people talk of 'class' you can detect a tendency to identify 'class' with *species*. Since you can delineate the *species* rabbit or tiger, it seems to those people that it should likewise be possible to delineate the *species* 'middle-class person'. They feel a duty to produce a portrait or identikit of such a person, to stand for and represent the whole class. This you could call the 'species-fallacy'. There is a rich example in that famous speech of Lord Brougham of 7 October 1831:

But if there is the mob, there is the people also. I speak now of the middle classes—of those hundreds of thousands of respectable persons—the most numerous, and by far the most wealthy order in the community; for if your Lordships' castles, manors, rights of warren and rights of chase, with all

your broad acres, were brought to the hammer, and sold at fifty years' pur-
chase, the price would fly up and kick the beam when counterpoised by the
vast and solid riches of those middle classes, who are also the genuine
depositaries of sober, rational, intelligent, and honest English feeling.
Unable though they may be to round a period or point an epigram, they are
solid right-judging men, and above all, not given to change. If they have a
fault, it is that error on the right side, a suspicion of state quacks—a dogged
love of existing institutions—a perfect contempt for all political nostrums.
They will neither be led astray by false reasoning, nor deluded by impudent
flattery; but so neither will they be scared by a classical quotation, or brow-
beaten by fine sentences; and as for an epigram, they care as little for it as
they do for a cannon ball. Grave—intelligent—rational—fond of thinking
for themselves—they consider a subject long before they make up their
minds on it; and the opinions they are thus slow to form they are not swift to
abandon.[9]

The dear man is plainly making it all up, under the delusion that, if
'middle classes' is a legitimate term, there must be some such person
walking the earth as a typical middle-class man. (Not, of course,
Brougham himself, who was very conscious of being 'Brougham of
Brougham Hall' and was busy remodelling his home in the style of a
medieval castle.) It is an absurd procedure and gives colour to the
views of those who regard the 'middle class'—at any rate at this
period—as a phantasm. For instance Kitson Clark, who cites 'two
words' which, he believes, 'have done more to stultify thought about
Victorian England than anything else':

They are the words 'middle class' . . . the whole weary range of phrases
which have become normal in any description of England at any period of
the nineteenth century—'the rising middle class', 'the predominant middle
class', 'middle-class taste', and perhaps above all 'middle-class morality' . . . Nor have the writers of text books, nor I am afraid many of the
teachers in schools, abandoned that curious legend that the middle class
came to dominate politics and the country immediately after the Reform Bill
of 1832 and remained in control till, presumably, the working classes took
over—but those who write in this way are normally a little vague on that
point.[10]

'Class' as a transaction

What I am trying to do is to open up the concept of 'class' and suggest the wealth of rhetorical complexities it offers. Let us consider
the rise of the notion of 'middle class'. It has a sort of ancestor in the
concept of the 'middle station' or 'middle fortune' in life. David

Hume wrote an essay in praise of 'The Middle Station of Life', and Robinson Crusoe's father lectured Crusoe on the same theme.

He told me . . . that mine was the middle state, or what might be called the upper station of low life, which he had found, by long experience, was the best state in the world, the most suited to human happiness; not exposed to the miseries and hardships, the labour and sufferings, of the mechanic part of mankind, and not embarrassed with the pride, luxury, ambition, and envy of the upper part of mankind . . .'[11]

The term 'station' begins to give way to 'class' in the mid-century—'the middling class' is used by Samuel Richardson in *Clarissa* (1748)—and by the 1790s this phrase and the phrase 'the middle classes' begin to be quite popular. At this early stage what tends to be implied is a distinctly humble sphere of life, not far removed from that of the 'common people'. (Mary Wollstonecraft writes: 'I pay particular attention to those in the middle class, because they appear to be in the most natural state.')[12] Soon, however, the term was taken up, very influentially, by James Mill. The whole thrust of Mill's political career was to urge the claims of the 'Middle Class'—the class which, he says, 'is universally described as both the most warm and the most virtuous part of the community',[13] and the class (this is important) of which he himself proudly claims to be a member. It is from Mill that Lord Brougham derived the theory, so important in the Reform Bill agitation, of the eminent virtue of the 'middle class'; and the use of the phrase as a rallying-cry survives till the time of Cobden, who describes himself and his allies in the Anti-Corn Law League as 'a middle-class set of agitators'.[14]

It is an interesting history, too sketchily treated here.[15] But the point that matters for my present purpose is that, or so it would appear, 'the middle class' is a purely middle-class concept. 'Middle-class' people talk about 'the working class', but—at any rate in this formative period—'working-class' people do not talk about 'the middle class'. If I am not mistaken, one can read all the nine hundred pages of E. P. Thompson's *The Making of the English Working Class* without once encountering a radical worker who invokes a 'middle class'; all his fire will be levelled at 'tyrants', 'the fiend aristocracy', 'placemen' and 'Old Corruption'. A mass of significance lurks in this fact. It reminds us, once again, of the deeply *conceptual* nature of the 'middle class', 'upper class' and 'working class'. We are not to imagine that people in the 1820s simply looked out of the window and *saw* these things in the world around them. They are primarily ideas, ideas in a logical relation to one another, and this relationship is an unsymmetrical one. We have in this last an important clue to the structure of the concept 'class'. By introspection we soon discern a basic law, i.e. that a 'working-class' person can become 'middle-class', indeed that is how there comes to be a 'middle class'; but a 'middle-class' person cannot become 'working-class'—though if change or disaster overtakes a 'middle-class' family, its children may well be born into the 'working class'. There are other such structural laws. Thus when I describe 'class' terminology as 'rhetorical', I do not mean that it has no intellectual content; but by the time we have identified all these laws we shall not be tempted to consider 'class' a simple concept.

Among the most helpful things written on 'class' and 'class'-language are Raymond Williams's articles on 'Class', 'Bourgeois' etc. in his *Keywords* (1976). Williams is strong on the structure of class ideas. However, running through these articles, there is a note almost of lament at the ambiguity, the 'difficulty' and the 'confusion' attending the use of these words. What this shows, I would want to suggest, is that he is looking for the wrong thing. He points out that English 'class'-language exhibits relics of two conflicting conceptions or models. There was the Upper/Middle/Lower model; and on the other hand the Saint-Simonian model, according to which 'both the self-conscious *middle classes* and the quite different people who by the end of the period would describe themselves as the *working classes* adopted the descriptions *useful* or *productive classes*, in distinction from and in opposition to the *privileged* or the *idle*'. And this use as he says, 'sorts oddly with the other model of *lower*, *middle* and *higher*' and has 'remained both important and confusing'. There were by now two common terms, increasingly used for comparison, distinction or contrast, which had been formed within quite different models:

On the one hand *middle* implied hierarchy and therefore implied 'lower class': not only theoretically but in repeated practice. On the other hand *working* implied productive or useful activity, which would leave all who were not 'working class' unproductive and useless (easy enough for an aristocracy, but hardly accepted by a productive 'middle class'). To this day this confusion reverberates.

Well, we can admit the *complication* all right. But what one wants to say, somehow, is: if a 'confusion' is purposeful or convenient, can it be properly called a confusion? I will come to my most general and crude point at once. Such terms, and the way they are used, are—as

I have said—rhetorical. That is to say, their *raison d'être* is, under a disguise, to further certain purposes or desires. We have to forget any idea that 'classes' 'really' exist. They are not that sort of thing, but rather fictions or imaginary frames that people project upon others, and these will differ of necessity according to who is doing the projecting and why; moreover the same people will construct these frames differently in different contexts and under the pressure of different circumstances.

It follows that the idea that 'classes' can be defined by economic or material *criteria*, or indeed *defined* by criteria at all, is a mistake. Fairly plainly—though there are those, even rather absurdly some sociologists, who seem to assume otherwise—describing people as 'middle class' or 'working class' or 'upper class' is not just a matter of definition. Those who use these phrases do not merely mean that certain people, by fulfilling certain conditions (of form of employment, income, birth, choice of marriage-partners, education, accent, etc.) are *by definition* 'middle class' or 'working class' or 'upper class' (as you might say that somebody who is wholly the property of another is by definition a slave, or somebody who disbelieves in the divinity of Christ is by definition a Socinian). If there were no more to it than that, no one would ever get heated on the subject, or even be much interested by it. What is being asserted by these phrases, rather, is the existence of a group of people possessing something deeply in common—of which similarity of form of employment, or income, or birth, choice of marriage-partners, education, accent, etc. is merely a *sign*. (What kind of thing they are supposed to have in common will of course differ very widely according to the speaker: for a Marxist it is a destiny, for others it is a culture.)

Thus the point is, to assign people to the 'middle class', or the 'working class' or the 'upper class' is a judgement and a speculation, and these will inevitably be coloured by who is doing the judging and the speculating and with what motive. The truth is, users of these terms demand a vast, and quite 'unscientific', freedom of manœuvre. It may be a very strong card to play, politically speaking, to include, or *not* to include, such-and-such people within a certain 'class' (the class you claim to belong to, or the class whose interests you claim to be defending, or the class you are attacking), and you will not lightly give up the right to be inconsistent on the matter and to delimit the classes differently in different circumstances. Nor is the case much different when the terms are being used in a non-political and 'purely social' sense, as when one speaks

or thinks of others in terms of 'class-distinction'. The user of them
will still be claiming a freedom. He will be reserving the right to pass
judgement, on purely inward and non-material grounds, that so-
and-so, *whatever* his wealth or position, 'does not belong to our class'.

Let me put it another way: to use 'class' terminology is always,
and in the nature of things, to engage in a social *transaction*. Thus if
you assign someone to a 'class', you are thereby and *ipso facto* assigning yourself and your listeners to some 'class' also. To use 'class' terminology is a social *act* and (notionally anyway) is to enter into
social relations with others. Further, in the case at least of the English 'class'-system, it is to engage in value-judgement. For what is it
but a social value-judgement to pronounce about others or yourself
that they are socially 'higher' or 'lower', are 'upper class' or 'middle
class' or 'lower' (or 'working') class? (It is these facts, as I shall
argue later, which should cause a historian or a sociologist to fight
shy of such terms; for how can it be for historians or sociologists to
be passing social value-judgements?)

We have only told half the story, though, when we say that using
'class'-language is a transaction. Equally important is the fact that
people who use such language tend instinctively to talk as if they
were neutral observers—as if, by some strange and special dispen-
sation, they and their hearers stood outside the 'class'-system. Here
comes in the significance of the gesture which the word 'class' makes
to scientific classification or taxonomy. We should be clear that it is
only a gesture; for in taxonomy there is no scope for an individual to
opt out of the system (or for an ostrich to take a holiday from his
family the *Struthionidae*). Nevertheless it is a potent gesture, seeming
to move the discussion towards the 'value-free' and 'scientific'. It is,
indeed, precisely the basis of many subtle transactions.

As an example of this opting-out I will take a page or two from
Donald Davie's autobiographical study *These the Companions* (1982)
in which Davie analyses his own social origins. He writes:

Barnsley society, as it was known to a schoolboy, was rigorously simplified
and, as I see now, truncated: there were only two classes—proletarian and
petty bourgeois. Solicitors, clergymen, doctors (though not dentists) sent
their children away to boarding-schools; and so, effectively, in St Mary's
School there were only the sons of colliers and the sons of small shopkeepers
like my father.[16]

Next he discusses his family's political loyalties, which were Tory in
an overwhelmingly Labour borough. He notes: 'I have indulged the

notion that, growing up thus in a disfranchised minority, and learning at my mother's knee the inevitable tension between us the few and them the many, I was conditioned to a political attitude that used to be called *poujadiste*; and I have fancied that I detected in myself the sentiments of a petty bourgeois Fascist.' Against this he is able to cite a memorable dream, which he had forty years later in California, in which a collier figured as a good Samaritan and protector. He welcomes this dream, he says, because it disproves his fears about his own attitudes. 'Perhaps it even disproves the Marxist theory of classes.' He continues:

both my grandmothers had been domestic servants. To be sure they had all 'bettered themselves', and though I don't remember that expression being used in my childhood, plainly the idea behind it was still potent in my parents' generation, and even indeed in my own. How ingrained it is in the English, and how tediously mean minded, this game of class-distinctions! I'm ashamed to find it is a game that I still play myself, as these comments show.[17]

We have here, to my mind, a rich example of a certain kind of writing about 'class' and of a subtle temptation that one can also detect in one's own heart. It is most serious, intelligent and sophisticated—yet at the same time, if you reflect on it, how devious! (The word sounds too pejorative, but I can find no better.) At each point the author occupies territory only to retreat from it. He specifies 'classes' in his childhood but quietly puts aside the question, to what 'class' does he belong now? (Perhaps we are to think, since he now lives in America, that he belongs to none?) Again, he makes use of Marxist 'class' terminology, then gently and quizzically disowns it, as very possibly 'disproved'. Finally he stigmatizes the whole business of 'class-distinctions' as a 'game', and 'mean minded', though it is a game that he is still playing. And we reflect that, in so condemning it, he is playing the game even harder and at a further remove. 'Game' does seem the right word; and most complex are the rules of this game. It is these rules that I am keen to elucidate.

It makes it easier to explore them if we turn to the earlier nineteenth century. For the game, then, was new, and skill in playing it had not yet become instinctive; so that its pioneers play it particularly boldly—and, if you like, outrageously. They were, moreover, less constricted even than thinkers of today by what one might call the 'belonging question'. If you think of, say, James Mill and Cobden and Matthew Arnold—all addicted to invoking the 'middle class' or 'middle classes'—it is not to be supposed they would have agreed, even within very wide limits, as to who actually belonged to the 'middle class' or 'middle classes'.* Indeed we need hardly suppose that, in using these terms, this membership problem was in the forefront of their minds at all, or that in their heads, when they used these terms, there arose any very vivid picture of actual faces or suits of clothes, or any clear-cut list of occupations. The definition, in this sense, of the 'working class' would have been almost equally elastic. No two speakers would have agreed as to which kind of shopkeeper or technician belonged to it; and those, in search of a 'pure' working class, who asserted that *no* shopkeeper, *no* clerk, *no* technician belonged to it, would still not have been in any agreement or have found their true working class. As for the 'upper class', it was from this membership point of view vagueness itself—except that, presumably, most dukes and earls belonged to it.

Thus we see particularly clearly in writers of this earlier period how the game is played. Someone invokes, say, the 'middle class': he describes it as solid, sagacious and honest, and incapable of classical quotations (Brougham); or as cruel, exploitative, and self-deceivingly idealistic (Engels); or as full of 'the hardness and vulgarity of middle-class liberalism . . . the hideous and grotesque illusions of middle-class Protestantism' (Matthew Arnold); or as cultured, altruistic, and high-minded, free from the vices of populace and peers (Matthew Arnold again). For such invocations to have force politically, it is not necessary to imagine that there was or is some object out there in Britain with which these portrayals could be compared for accuracy. It is not cynicism but simple common sense to say that the language of 'class' does not function in that way—any more than, shall we say, the language of religion.

There is a nice illustration of this point in Matthew Arnold's *Culture and Anarchy* (1869). Having flayed the 'middle class' for its

---

* Guizot, addressing the French Chamber of Deputies in 1837, was commendably frank in this respect:

> Have I assigned any limits to the middle class? Have you heard me say where it begins or where it ends? I have carefully abstained from doing this: I have distinguished neither a superior class, nor inferior classes: I have simply expressed the generalisation that there exists, in the bosom of a great country like France, a class which is not bound to manual labour, which does not live from wages, which has the leisure to think, which can consecrate a considerable part of its time and its faculties to public affairs, which has not only the wealth necessary for such work, but which has, at the same time, enlightenment and independence, without which this work cannot be accomplished . . .
>
> (*Le Moniteur universel*, 5 and 6 May 1837; trans. C. Emsley)

'hideous and grotesque illusions' and having named its members as 'Philistines', he turns round and offers himself as an example of the class ('my own class, the middle class, with which I am in closest sympathy')—albeit as a 'defective' member of it.

> I shall leave the defect of aristocracy unillustrated by any representative man. But with oneself one may always, without impropriety, deal quite freely; and indeed, this sort of plain-dealing with oneself has in it, as all the moralists tell us, something very wholesome. So I will venture to humbly offer myself as an illustration of defect in those forces and qualities which make our middle class what it is. The too well-founded reproaches of my opponents declare how little I have lent a hand to the great works of the middle class . . . [18]

Of course Arnold is a professional wag, and on this 'class' business he is openly juggling with paradoxes. But he did not invent the paradoxes, they are inherent in the game.

A similar having-it-all-ways game is played even more explicitly by Thackeray in his *Book of Snobs* (1848). The fictitious scourge of snobs who is supposedly writing the book claims to belong to the 'middle ranks' of society but is at pains to defeat the reader's efforts to 'place' him socially: at one moment we learn he is a commonplace domestic sort of person, living in Somer's Town with a wife Bessy with 'jolly mottled arms' and a household full of her hungry relatives, at another we find he is a clubman and an associate of dukes. The major theme of the book, as its full title *The Book of Snobs: by One of Themselves* suggests, presents a related paradox, much of the joke lying in a sort of endless mirror-image recession, by which an obsession with snobbery is represented as itself snobbish. ' . . . have I not said before', writes the author, 'that I should be ready to jump out of my skin if two Dukes would walk down Pall Mall with me?'

It is important to realize what a remarkable and profound invention it was, the concept of the 'snob' and 'snobbery'. It is one that is unknown in this form to other cultures; and so far as I can see, Thackeray invented it more or less single-handed. In his undergraduate days he edited a magazine called *The Snob*, in which the term 'snob', which literally means 'cobbler', was undergraduate slang for 'vulgar' or 'low-bred'. Thus the staple fare of the magazine was Gown v. Town humour: jokes about 'common' accents and misspellings and extracts from the 'Proceedings of the Seven Dials Parliament'. It was shame at this episode of his unregenerate and 'barbarian' youth which lay behind *The Book of Snobs* of sixteen years later, in which the abusive term 'snob' is not rejected but is transferred to, or reversed upon, those who would use it in that sense. According to his new theory, the vulgarest thing (sense 2) you can do is to look down on somebody for being vulgar (sense 1) or to curry favour with somebody for being non-vulgar. The two essential features of the concept are the one mentioned above, viz., that there is no exit from the trap, for to concern yourself with snobbery is snobbish; and that for the first time there is a term which equates servility towards those 'above' you with arrogance towards those 'below' you. (Thus there is at last a single word to define Jane Austen's Mr Collins.)

The new concept was in a sense called forth by the moment. In the early 1840s a chorus of voices was complaining of 'flunkeyism' and social climbing as a nationwide epidemic. The complaints, however, tended to be confused and in bad faith. Thus Bulwer Lytton, in *England and the English*, severely castigates the 'aristocratic contagion' which infects England and 'extends from the highest towards the verge of the lowest'.[19] A year or two before, in his novel *The Disowned* (1829) he had given a rancorous caricature of the Copperases, a grotesque City stockjobber and his wife, keepers of a genteel lodging house ('Copperas Bower') in Paddington. The portrait is plainly intended as a general assault on the 'middle class' and its vulgarity; and the chapter in which the Copperases are introduced has as its epigraph an aristocratic sneer from a certain (imaginary?) Stephen Montague: 'The middle classes are of all the most free from the vices of conduct, and the most degraded by the meannesses of character.' It required Thackeray's concept of 'snobbery' to pinpoint the self-contradiction in these attitudes of Lytton's: that his rancour against the Copperases is a reflex of his own 'silver-fork' pretensions, and he is caught in the 'snobbery' trap. Interestingly, in a later revision of *England and the English* Lytton made use of Thackeray's word 'snobbery',[20] and in later editions of *The Disowned* the rawest anti-'middle class' gibes have disappeared.

This said, and brilliant as Thackeray's theory of 'snobbery' was, it remains true that it was to some extent a game: this indeed is what gives it a tinge of perversity, that perversity we are always so conscious of in Thackeray and which weakened him as an artist. No doubt Thackeray did not seriously consider himself a snob (though plenty of others considered him one). Similarly, neither he nor Matthew Arnold would seriously have assigned themselves to the 'middle class', any more than they would have assigned themselves to the 'upper class'. The concept which really mattered to them was 'gentleman' (and 'no-gentleman'). Anyway it was bad manners to talk about your 'class'. The point was rather that there were manœuvres to be performed by means of these concepts. A leading rule of the game is that, immediately you start using 'class' terms as epithets (as in 'a typical middle-class attitude', and so on), you draw attention right away from the 'belonging' question—the question of who does and who does not belong to the class in question. While Arnold is flaying the 'middle class' (or indeed when Roland Barthes is flaying the 'bourgeoisie') it never occurs to us to ask what class *they* belong to. For they are talking to *us*, and if we are listening to them assentingly we will unconsciously assume that, whatever class they belong to, we belong to it also.

We can find another instructive example in Richard Cobden, so famous as the advocate of 'middle-class' power in Britain. In his utterances it is left deliberately unclear whom the 'middle class' or 'middle classes' comprise; and whether they *do* now hold the levers of power in Britain, or merely *ought* to; and whether or not he regards himself as belonging to it (or them). In an early pamphlet *England, Ireland and America* (1835) he performs a somewhat Arnoldian trick of self-inculpation. He has been praising the American republican constitution and asks whether it should be imitated in Britain. No, is his answer. For the entire British population, from peer to chimney-sweeper, has a hopeless addiction to aristocracy, an 'insatiable love of caste'. Where would be the advantage if 'we of the middle class', who are 'more enslaved than any other to this passion', were to overthrow the 'lofty patricians'? It would merely mean erecting an even more ignoble aristocracy, an aristocracy of wealth.

Here, for polemical and ironical purposes, Cobden is claiming membership of the 'middle class'. On a different occasion, the Corn Law debate of 17 February 1843, he wins moral capital by describing himself as 'a farmer's son',[21] with the implication that he is *not* of the 'middle class'. He writes to his brother Frederick (11 March 1843) of how this declaration of his lowly birth has actually done his reputation good with the 'middle class'.

By the way, it is a wholesome sign that my middle-class popularity seems rather to be increased by my avowal of my origin; and for the first time probably a man is served by that aristocratic class, who owes nothing to birth, parentage, patronage, connexions, or education. Don't listen to the nonsense about our being prosecuted. The enemy has burnt his fingers already by meddling with the Leaguers. Wait till we have held two or three

weekly meetings in Drury Lane Theatre, and you will see that we are not the
men to be put to the ordeal of a middle-class jury.[22]

Here the 'middle class' acquires the sobriquet 'aristocratic', and a
'middle-class jury' is made to signify a jury drawn from Cobden's
class-enemies.

In an often-quoted passage, Cobden says that circumstances
(meaning difficulties with the Chartists) 'have, to a considerable
extent, compelled us to make our agitation a middle-class agitation'.

I do not deny that the working classes generally have attended our lectures
and signed our petitions; but I will admit, that so far as the fervour and
efficiency of our agitation has gone, it has eminently been a middle-class agitation. We have had our meetings of dissenting ministers, we have obtained
the co-operation of the ladies; we have resorted to tea-parties, and taken
those pacific means for carrying out our views, which mark us rather as a
middle-class set of agitators.[23]

Historians like to cite this passage as evidence about the 'middle
class' in the 1840s, but they tend to ignore an essential point, viz.,
that Cobden is being equivocal, and deriving advantage from being
equivocal, about whether he himself is of the 'middle class'. It was
reliance on such or similar equivocations which emboldened Cobden to take one of the most extraordinary steps of his career. In June
1846, only a few months after Peel's famous *volte-face* over the Corn
Laws, it became known that Peel was contemplating resignation, as
a result of a defeat over his Irish policy. Hearing this, Cobden wrote
his old enemy a long personal letter, to be burnt after reading,
attempting to dissuade him. It held before Peel's eyes, as it were, a
magical *Tarnhelm* or Nibelung ring, ensuring success, in the shape of
representativeness of the 'middle class'.

I will not speak of the populace, which to a man is with you; but of the active
and intelligent middle classes, with whom you have engrossed a sympathy
and interest greater than was ever before possessed by a minister . . . You
represent the IDEA of the age, and it has no other representative amongst
statesmen . . . Do you shrink from the post of governing through the *bona
fide* representatives of the middle class? Look at the facts, and can the
country be otherwise ruled at all? There must be an end of the juggle of parties, the mere representatives of traditions, and some man must of necessity
rule the State through its governing class . . . Are you afraid of the middle
class? You must know them better than to suppose that they are given to
extreme or violent measures. They are not democratic.[24]

In his grateful reply Peel, not too unexpectedly, made no reference
at all to the 'middle class'.

If 'class'-language, as I have been arguing, has proved in practice to be a 'game' and a transaction, the question now arises,
what attitude should be taken to it by a historian or a sociologist?
It seems plain that *as* a historian or sociologist (whatever is true of
him as a citizen) he will never be able to take on Arnold and
Thackeray at this linguistic game: their footwork is too nimble,
their tactics are altogether too advanced. Anyway, if to use 'class'
terms involves a social transaction, such terms can hardly be for a
historian to use—for how can he have social relations with the
dead? However, it may be objected: if the ordinary-life usage
'class' is no use to him, this may be precisely what is wrong with
it. It is too clever, in a vicious sort of way, and the historian must
seek something more plodding—something simpler, purer and
'scientific'.

For instance like the Marxist one. But then you think of the
Marxist one, and it does not seem all that pure and simple. At all
events this usage, too, plainly involves a *transaction*. The task Marx is
concerned with when speaking of 'classes' is not that of identifying
'classes' but that of bringing 'classes' into being. His life-aim is to
create a proletariat, a proletariat with revolutionary consciousness,
and all means are permissible towards that end. The problem is to
make the underprivileged think of themselves as a 'class', the proletariat; and an essential aid in this will be to flesh out an enemy for
this 'class', viz., another 'class', the 'bourgeoisie'. These 'classes' are
necessary fictions which it is Marx and the Marxists' aim to make
come true. And meanwhile, to help the present, the Marxist historian will try out these fictions on the past. I think it is legitimate to
speak of this too as a transaction with society. It would hardly occur
to you to tackle the unpromising task of interpreting the English
Civil War, or the Punic Wars, in terms of 'class-struggle' unless you
had a strong *wish* for the 'class-struggle' to be real, to continue and
to be won.

I cannot immediately see a way out for the historian or sociologist.
However he uses 'class' terms, whether according to everyday usage
or according to the Marxist one, they deprive him of the neutrality
or objectivity which we suppose him to cherish. Marx cannot, any
more than we, detach himself from his own society when using these
terms—except by an extreme measure, which is to detach himself
from humanity altogether. And, great humanist as he was, this is a
step he sometimes seems to be tempted by. It must be in some such
spirit that he can rest the hopes of humanity on 'the complete loss of

man'[25]—that is to say on the worsening and taking to the extreme of dereliction of the position of the worker.

I shall come back to these questions. Meanwhile, if you accept that 'class' and a 'class-system' have, as concepts, the peculiar nature that I describe, then you need to approach them in an appropriate frame of mind. I mean, it hardly seems sensible to condemn them for 'difficulty'. We would *expect* them to be difficult—to be difficult and cunning in their *use*, just in proportion to their apparent simplicity of *form*. When I say this, I am intending no special attack on Raymond Williams and his wish that things could be less 'confused', less difficult,[26] for the same reflection teases us often when we are reading social historians.

Nor does it tease one only when they are writing about 'class'. The same puzzle arises for us when they are writing about other and more traditional social categories and social 'systems'. I will quote Colin Lucas, in an article 'Nobles, Bourgeois and the French Revolution'.

One may suggest that the confusion of the Ancien Régime social scene is largely due to the fact that the mechanisms of social ascension were extremely delicate. They demanded constant vigilance and a fine judgement.[27]

By 'confusion' Lucas means the difficulty (for us) in distinguishing 'nobles' (*nobles*) from 'bourgeois' in France in the mid-eighteenth century. There was, he is arguing, a property-owning élite, but within this élite 'noble' versus 'bourgeois' was not a significant division. (Nor was the 'bourgeoisie' a politically conscious 'class'—it only became so as a *result* of the French Revolution). 'Noble' and 'bourgeois' were both very flexible terms, and 'At the end of the *Ancien Régime*, rank in the upper reaches of society was far too subtle a notion to be confined within the ungainly corsetry of nobles versus commoners.' Yes, but 'confusion'? It is not plain why, because there were 'delicate mechanisms' of social ascension in eighteenth-century France, we need regard the system as 'confused' (though we may find it confusing—just as we may find it vicious). Complicated it evidently was. But then why should we expect it to be simple? Of course it would have been in the interest of some members of that élite to describe it all in simple terms, but (need I say?) it is not for social historians to believe them. Then a page or two later in Lucas's article we see the corollary of his notion of 'confusion': I mean, the notion that at an earlier period things were unconfused and orderly—and not only orderly, but simpler. There had been a time, and this time had not yet quite gone, when 'Frenchmen still accepted that nobility was the purest expression of social superiority. They accepted, as the medieval world had accepted, that it reflected virtue.'[28] This is indeed a hallowed belief, but it sounds most implausible.

Aspect

As I said earlier, in classing someone socially, one is simultaneously classing oneself, and if one person speaks to another about 'class' he or she is *ipso facto* creating a tacit understanding with the other about their relative class position. Now, this raises the important question, that I have already touched on, of *aspect*: that is to say whether, or how, things take a different appearance according to who is speaking. Engels, in *The Condition of the Working Class in England*, says that, from the point of view of the worker, there was no visible difference between the landowning gentry and 'middle-class' manufacturers. It is in this context, I mean seeing things from the worker's point of view, that Engels is formulating the term 'bourgeoisie' in the new political-theory sense, the one so vastly influential when taken over by Marx—i.e. as denoting the whole 'ruling class' (the class set over against the 'proletariat'). In the chapter 'The Attitude of the Bourgeoisie' Engels writes:

When I speak here of the Bourgeoisie, I am including the so-called Aristocracy, for this latter is only an aristocracy, it is only privileged, in relation to the Bourgeoisie, not in relation to the Proletariat. The Proletariat sees in both simply property-owners, that is to say 'bourgeois'. All other privileges disappear from sight in the face of the privilege of property-ownership.[29]

I shall come later to this important topic, of how Marx and Engels performed the strange feat of imposing the term 'bourgeois' upon intellectuals as the name for the *whole* 'ruling class'. Meanwhile, my point is that what Engels was saying here was very reasonable. Early nineteenth-century working people were quite justified in not distinguishing the 'middle class' from the 'upper class': the distinction truly and logically did not exist from their angle of view. And, to take another case, if we turn to the later nineteenth century, when the distinction between 'upper middle class' and 'lower middle class' had arisen, the question of 'aspect' is again all-important. For to the landed gentry this distinction 'upper middle class'/'lower middle class' would simply not have been meaningful: it would (again quite

truly and logically) not have existed. 'Upper middle class' and
'lower middle class' are concepts meaningful only for those who
believe, or hope, that they belong to the 'upper middle class'. And
no one ever, except for purposes of irony, called himself or herself
'lower middle class'; it is a concept purely for others. (People may
say that they were *born* into the 'lower middle class', but that will
mean precisely that they no longer belong to it.) Moreover, let us not
tell ourselves that these terms 'upper middle class' and 'lower
middle class' are frivolous and unreal, as opposed to the 'reality' of
the terms 'working class', 'middle class', and 'upper class'. All these
concepts are roughly on a level; they are pictures of society taken
from a particular angle and are only meaningful from that angle.
Thus there are several patterns and systems here, according to who
is speaking, and these patterns do not coincide. The result is a jarring or oscillation, like the one in that interview with Lady Longford, and such as we encounter twenty times a day.

2
*
The 'bourgeoisie'

In studying the rise of 'class' there is a fact that we should not forget: it is that we are, essentially, talking about Britain. The term in its new sense—the sense according to which there is a class 'system' and in which people assign themselves and others to a 'class' and use 'class' names as a rallying cry or as a social criterion—did not for a long time achieve anything like the same popularity in France. It is true that by the mid-eighteenth century the term *classe*, with its 'enlightened' and non-hierarchical connotations, had become widely used in France in a socio-economic sense, as a rival to more traditional and mystical terms such as *état* and *ordre*. Thus the physiocrat Quesnay, in his *Analyse* (1766), divided the nation into 'three classes of citizens: the productive class, the class of proprietors, and the sterile class'; and Turgot propounded a rather similar scheme. The implications of the term, however, tended to be left latent or vague and were not used as the basis of a new theory of society.[1] This indeed remained broadly true long after the Revolution, there being nothing resembling the new situation in Britain, in which a class-'system' of upper/middle/lower came to acquire contentious and emotive significance for ordinary people. 'As late as 1848', writes William H. Sewell Jr. in *Work and Revolution* (1980), 'the term "class", and even the term "working-class" remained simply a descriptive designation in France':

'proletarian' or 'aristocrat' or 'association' carried powerful political and emotional charges, but 'class' did not. The term *classe* was alien to the moralistic and utopian temper of French workers' movements throughout the July monarchy.

. . . 'Class loyalty' would have sounded reprehensible to workers in 1848: it would have implied a loyalty to some selfish interest as against the common interest . . . It was no accident that workers' consciousness in 1848 was more attuned to words that emphasised unity—like 'association'—than to words that emphasised distinctions like 'class'.[2]

The phenomenon in France that corresponds much more closely to the rise of the concept 'class' is a different one. It is the revival of the word 'bourgeois'. The term 'bourgeois' had been on everybody's lips under the *ancien régime* in France, but at the French Revolution it had dropped into silence—and for very good reason, for, just as much as 'noble', it smelled much too dangerously of the old order. Thus, when eventually the word came out from under its ban, the re-defining of it offered rich and varied opportunities.

Among those laying greedy hands upon the word was Claude-Henri de Saint-Simon. In the eyes of Saint-Simon the Revolution had not borne fruit; it had failed to enthrone the worker (*industriel*) or to inaugurate the harmonious reign of Science and Industry. And this, he concluded, was because it had been betrayed—betrayed even at the time—by a group of false friends (Girondins, Jacobins and Bonapartists) to whom the workers had unwisely entrusted their cause, instead of fighting for it themselves. This small but dangerous group, according to Saint-Simon, was really no more than an offshoot of feudalism. And he tried out various names for it, légistes, *avocats*, metaphysicians, 'the Bonapartist feudality', or 'the intermediate class'—before, in 1823, settling upon the name '*bourgeois*'.[3]

Now this verbal manœuvre of Saint-Simon's was in entire contrast with Liberal opinion in France. For the French Liberal thinkers the old 'virtuous' associations of the word 'bourgeois' ('le bon bourgeois': the *good* bourgeois, etc.) were uppermost, and they applied the name, not like Saint-Simon to a small group, but to the industrious majority of the nation. (The historian Thierry actually equated the 'bourgeoisie' with the whole body of the workers.)

Thus, in the 1820s, the word 'bourgeois' was all adrift from its *ancien régime* moorings and a rich booty for whoever could capture it; and soon, as we know, it was decisively commandeered by Marx—or shall we say, shared out between Marx and Flaubert. This was a most important event, but before considering it, I must sketch the earlier history of the word (or the concept) 'bourgeois'.

We may begin in the sixteenth century, when the word is quite uncontroversial and exhibits an orderly array of senses. Its medieval, and etymological, sense is 'town-dweller', i.e. inhabitant of a *bourg*; and this sense is still active in the sixteenth century. A town-dweller could still, by paying dues and fulfilling certain conditions, acquire special legal status, which entitled him to various privileges and immunities; and the name for this status was *bourgeoisie*—one applied for and obtained *lettres de bourgeoisie* and had one's name inscribed on the city's burgher-rolls.

The other senses of 'bourgeois' in the sixteenth century were natural extensions of the first.[4] The word could mean 'inhabitant' or 'denizen', or 'citizen' in the honorific *civis romanus* sense. Bodin's phrase for a 'Roman citizen' is *bourgeois romain*, and Calvin speaks of *bourgeois du ciel* ('citizens of heaven'). There was no automatically implied opposition to *noble*, and a nobleman might apply to become the bourgeois of a city.

In the seventeenth century the word 'bourgeois' suffers its first major vicissitude. The word, in its adjectival form, grows controversial, and in certain contexts and on the lips of certain speakers, becomes a sneer. What seems to have happened is that the nobility, finding themselves tamed and humiliated by Richelieu and Mazarin, decided to take out their resentment on the non-noble. (They were further aggrieved by the fact that in 1614 *noblesse de robe*, i.e. nobility conferred on holders of high legal office, was made hereditary.) The earliest pejorative use of 'bourgeois' generally quoted occurs in Charles Sorel's novel *Vrai histoire comique de Francion* (1622)—where it is, precisely, presented as an example of court arrogance. ('He and his companions opened their mouth almost as one man to call me 'bourgeois', for that is the insult which that *canaille* court-pages hurl at those whom they regard as fools or as people who do not follow court manners.') This pejorative of the adjective 'bourgeois' grows common in the latter half of the century and reaches Richelet's *Dictionary* in 1680. It was at this time that the duc de Saint-Simon, in resentment at his fellow-courtiers (all of whom were noble, though of newer creation) called it an 'age of *vile bourgeoisie*'.

The question of the 'bourgeois' was, it would seem, intensely on people's mind at this time, at least in the environs of the court: the fact is plain from Molière's *Le Bourgeois Gentilhomme* (1670) and Antoine Furetière's novel *Le Roman bourgeois* (1666). One needs to remember that, at least until the move to Versailles in the 1680s, the French nobility were far from living an aloof and mandarin existence. For one thing, by English standards, nobles in France—who really corresponded to the 'nobility and gentry' in England—were as plentiful as blackberries. Noble and non-noble in France were continually in one another's company, so that any Gwendolen Fairfax-like assertion of ignorance of bourgeois ways on the part of nobles was a conscious fiction. Similarly there was never the same tendency in France as there was in Germany (for instance with Goethe and Hegel) to attribute deep philosophical virtues to 'nobility'. It was always, in France, an essentially worldly quality, and remained so

even when idealized, in fantastic and nostalgic fashion, by the nineteenth-century dandy.

I suspect that in the very influential 'noble' versus 'bourgeois'
clash that we have been discussing we should see an early example
of a phenomenon familiar in the twentieth century, a communal
rivalry at the purely 'social' level. Rivalry (this is my point) implies
a kind of equality; though in the present case the 'nobles' would
have been the last to admit such an equality, and the 'bourgeois'
also helped to obscure it by being ready to model themselves on the
'nobles'. Etiquette books of this period made much of the fact that
court speech-habits were distinguishable from 'bourgeois' ones.
'The bourgeois speak very differently from us,' says a spokesman in
François de Callières's *Mots à la mode* (1693), and in his *Du bon et du
mauvais usage* a little exemplary scene is presented in which the young
M. Thibault, the child of bourgeois parents, visits a noble house,
and the lady of the house kindly corrects his awkward and provincial
turns of phrase—like saying '*un mien ami*' instead of '*un de mes amis*' or
'*deffunt mon père*' (my deceased father) instead of '*feu mon père*' (my
late father). It would be wise, however, to repress the stock assumption or sneer that such books were written for social gate-crashers.
They are better regarded as courtly propaganda, and they were no
doubt read by the noble as much as by the bourgeois. Nor was
linguistic imitation a one-way affair. Courtly speech-habits filtered
down and became national ones, but (as the imaginary Duke in
Callières complains) the reverse also took place, and bourgeois
phrases invaded the court.[5]

There is a vivid picture of the rivalry I have been speaking of in
Furetière's *Le Roman bourgeois*. Furetière declares his intention to
write about ordinary folk: 'good people of mediocre condition, who
go quietly along their high-road'. And in fact, though the book is a
counterblast to high-flown romances in the style of *Clélie* or *Le Grand
Cyrus*, it is not a burlesque but a serious and quite talented novel. Its
theme, however, is almost wholly that of the rivalry, mutual mis-
apprehension and mutual exploitation of bourgeois and noble. His
tone is oddly unstable. He gives a sympathetic and rather touching
characterization to his bourgeoise heroine; yet he insists from time to
time, unconvincingly and as if on some polemical principle, that her
motives in angling for a noble suitor are purely materialistic. His
book was polemical in other respects also, and its 'lowness' got him
into trouble with his *noble* reading-public. The issue here was evidently to do with a kind of blowing the gaff. For Furetière the

meaning of the word 'bourgeois' is 'belonging to the kind of life we all know about and have a foot in, though we like to pretend we don't'.

There is a certain irony in the way that 'bourgeois', as an epithet, became pejorative. A favourite anti-'bourgeois' phrase came to be *'ça c'est du dernier bourgeois'* ('that is the very depth of bourgeoisity'), and this phrase originates in Molière's *Les Précieuses ridicules* (1659), where in fact it figures as an example of absurd and vulgar affection—of would-be exclusiveness on the part of very provincial and unaristocratic girls. This is indeed Molière's normal stance. The theme of his *Le Bourgeois Gentilhomme* is bourgeois good sense: the good sense and the decency of Mme Jourdain and her servant Nicolle as against the mad pretensions of M. Jourdain and the squalid rapacity of his noble parasites.

During the remainder of the *ancien régime* period the term 'bourgeois' continued to hold up its head against the term *noble*, so that it always remained possible to use it in an honorific sense. But indeed, as a result of the close intermingling of 'nobles' and 'bourgeois', the terms sometimes crossed their frontier in a curious fashion. Thus, according to Colin Lucas (he is referring to the period just before the Revolution): 'almost everywhere except in Normandy the appellation "noble" really meant a superior sort of non-noble'[6]. (Of course this verbal usage, 'so-and-so' to mean 'not really so-and-so, but just as good as if it were' is a familiar one, and we often meet it in advertising.) Again during the eighteenth century, in legal and fiscal contexts, there is growing use of the terms *bourgeois vivant bourgeoisement* (bourgeois living in bourgeois fashion) and *bourgeois vivant noblement* (bourgeois living in noble fashion), to denote a style of leisured *rentier* existence; and it perhaps confirms Colin Lucas's remark about 'noble' sometimes meaning not-noble that, so far as one can see, there is not much difference in meaning between the two phrases.

The next important event in the history of the term 'bourgeois' takes place in 1789, and it is a negative one—but none the less significant for that. The word 'bourgeois' suddenly drops into disuse. 'Aristocrate', 'citoyen', 'peuple': these were the significant terms of the French Revolution, and the terms 'noble' and 'bourgeois' were at a discount: and on the lips of French Revolutionary orators the word 'bourgeois' is heard very rarely.

The reason for this is not far to seek. If you are a member of the Constituent Assembly or the Convention and you want to identify and praise a counter-force to the aristocracy, you will inevitably

refer to the 'peuple' (the 'people'). You will not be on your honour to
specify whom the 'people' consists of. It suffices that, through the
centuries, people have agreed to speak abusively of the 'people', calling it (or them) 'base' and 'vile', 'dregs', 'rabble', etc.; it had been a
comfort to everyone, noble, bourgeois or peasant, to hypothesize a
group indisputably 'lower' than themselves, a group 'without
honour'. Hence, in 1789, generous feeling commands that you
should turn this mode of speech on its head and identify with, or at
least claim to speak for, this age-old victim, the 'people'. And on the
other hand, if you want to bestow blame on or point the finger of
accusation at enemies of Revolution, you will not lay this blame at
the door of the 'bourgeois'—for the reason that sneering at the
'bourgeois' is, notoriously, a disreputable aristocratic trait.

There is a curious example of this axiom in Robespierre. In 1793,
at the time of the counter-revolutionary risings in Marseilles, Lyons
and Bordeaux, Robespierre in a private memorandum[7] put the
blame upon the local 'bourgeois'.

The internal dangers come from the bourgeois; in order to defeat the bourgeois we must rally the people. Everything has been so disposed as to place
the people under the yoke of the bourgeois, and to send the defenders of the
Republic to the scaffold. They have triumphed at Marseilles, Bordeaux, and
Lyons; they would have triumphed in Paris too, but for the present insurrec-
tion.[8]

However, in his public utterances at the time, Robespierre made no
reference to the 'bourgeois' and levelled all his eloquence, as usual, at
'intriguers', 'the factious', 'despotism', and 'hydras'. Danton, at the
same period, characteristically referred to the counter-revolutionaries
in Marseilles as the 'aristocracy' of commerce ('The French nation
has just given a great lesson to the aristocracy of commerce')[9].

The word 'bourgeois', we see from this, had suddenly acquired an
archaic flavour, relating it to the *ancien régime*. The revolutionist Barère
has a nice story in his *Memoirs* about 'the Parisian bourgeois who positively insists on being noble and being banned from Paris'.

Amidst the severe measures taken against nobles, I presided over a scene in
the rue Saint-Honoré, at the hôtel de Savalette, of which a comic dramatist
might have been envious. A good Parisian of the *Marais*, son of an *échevin*
[something like a sheriff] of the municipality of Paris, came to consult me as
to whether he had to quit the capital and place himself under surveillance at
Passy. I replied that his nobility did not belong to that feudal nobility which

had lost everything at the Revolution and on which the suspicions of legislators were focused. However, the *bourgeois* of the *Marais* insisted on coming under the provisions of the law. I in turn insisted that he should stay with his family in Paris, repeating that such quite modern ennoblement as his was not in the least under threat. At this the Parisian *échevin* lost his temper before the largish company assembled there; he began to shout; he said he was as noble as any other noble in France—that the office of *échevin* carried with it a recognized and hereditary nobility. Hoping to calm him, and pretending to affirm the legitimacy of his rather untimely aristocratic pride, I offered to give him a certificate as *noble* and *lettré* authorized to stay in Paris.—'No, monsieur', he replied, 'I am not a man of letters. I am the son of an *échevin* of the city of Paris; I have to leave and I intend to leave in correct legal fashion.' He left the room in high rage.[10]

To Barère the 'bourgeois' versus 'noble' rivalry has already become merely quaint and nothing to do with *realpolitik*.

We are told by many historians, none the less, that the French Revolution was a 'bourgeois' revolution. It is worth questioning this. If we were to go by what the revolutionaries themselves said, and especially did not say, the 'bourgeois' scarcely came into it at all. Now of course one possible interpretation of this is that the revolutionaries knew they were bourgeois and wanted to hide it: they were bourgeois passing themselves off as the people as a whole (the people, that is to say, apart from the aristocrats). Another interpretation is that they were bourgeois but *didn't* know it; they really believed they were the 'peuple', and it is only in retrospect that it can be seen that they were bourgeois and were impelled by the sectional interests of the bourgeoisie—interests antagonistic to those of the non-bourgeois.

But these are not the only interpretations possible. You could also argue that, at the Revolution, the group of people who called themselves 'bourgeois', and were so called, disappeared as a group: the grouping was a product of the *ancien régime* and disappeared with the *ancien régime*. There is actually much to support this interpretation: viz., that the causes of the French Revolution are not to be sought in bourgeois frustrations or bourgeois political consciousness, but rather that the whole *ancien régime* system (characterized by a curious symbiosis of 'noble' and 'bourgeois') was hopelessly and dangerously antiquated and ripe for destruction, and that certain bourgeois and certain nobles realized the fact and resolved to overthrow it and put something better in its place. This is, broadly speaking, what the revolutionaries *said* happened—and perhaps after all, simple-minded though it may seem, we might actually go back to believing them?

It may be objected that the 'bourgeois' did not disappear for ever at the Revolution, and that at the Bourbon Restoration the *term* 'bourgeois', at least, came into constant use again—it was, for instance, never far from Balzac's pen. But what is important to note is that in Balzac the term 'bourgeois' is continually linked, more closely than ever before, with the term 'noble'. In his novels the 'bourgeois' or 'bourgeoises' are continually worrying about their social acceptance or otherwise by the nobility, and the nobility are preoccupied with lording it or queening it over the 'bourgeois'. Now, on the assumption that the French Revolution had been a 'bourgeois' one, this would seem very odd. If in 1789 the 'bourgeois' were a political class and as such defeated the aristocracy, and if Balzac's 'bourgeois' and 'bourgeoises' have any connection with that victorious class, why thirty years later are they currying favour with the aristocracy? It is not, surely, that the aristocracy have regained their old power? No doubt there were plenty of aristocrats about the place in the *Restauration* and later, indeed even under the July Monarchy they occupied most of the prominent government posts. Still, I think it would be agreed that the *ancien régime* had emphatically not returned and it was a new politico-economic scene altogether. What then do we make of this spectacle of the 'bourgeois' seeking the approval of their defeated enemy? Now, of course, an explanation would not be difficult. There would be nothing unexpected in the sight of the French people, in the private sphere—the sphere of the 'social' in the narrowest sense—performing *ancien régime* charades. Did not the well-to-do in Britain build themselves baronial castles? Yet they were scarcely hoping to restore feudalism. The return of a ghostly race of 'bourgeois' twinned with a ghostly nobility, in the France of the 1820s, would be in line with much that we know about the 'purely social'. 'Prestige', writes Proust, 'has to be imaginary to be efficacious.'

would not a society be secretly hierarchized in proportion as it became more democratic? It is perfectly possible. The political power of the Popes has grown greatly since they no longer rule states or possess an army; cathedrals had much less in the way of prestige for a seventeenth-century believer than they have for a twentieth-century atheist; and if the princesse de Parme had been sovereign of a state, no doubt I should have taken as much interest in talking about her as about the president of a republic, that is to say none at all.[11]

The only reason why this *salon* resuscitation of the term 'bourgeois' seems puzzling is because, at the same moment, social theorists like Saint-Simon were seizing on the ownerless word 'bourgeois' for quite other, and power-political, uses. The Saint-Simonians were agreed to blame the 'failure' of the Revolution on a small and malign group, still as active in the present day; and after searching about for a name for that group, they had perceived the advantage of the antiquated sobriquet of 'bourgeois'. The name 'bourgeois' was traditionally associated with sneers, albeit aristocratic sneers, so it was suitable to an enemy; and the fact that it was an outmoded name lent support to the theory that the group, under various disguises, had been exploiting France for many centuries. Whether recruited from the nobility or the plebs, they were the eternal idlers and parasites; and in their present incarnation they were typified by Liberalism, utilitarianism, economic *laissez-faire*, empiricism and (in literature) Romanticism.[12]

The Saint-Simonians were busy in 1830 and 1831 imposing their interpretation of the July Revolution as a victory for the bourgeoisie, ushering in a 'bourgeois' monarchy. Their definition of the 'bourgeois' as a small exploiting group was still in competition—so floating and unattached was the word 'bourgeois'—with the Liberals' quite different version, according to which the bourgeois were the working majority of the population. But within a few years their version won, and it was taken over by Marx, becoming central to his system.

One can date reasonably precisely the moment at which Marx adopted the French term *'bourgeois'*. It occurred in the last months of 1843, the time of his arrival in Paris and his first encounter with French workers' associations—the time, indeed, when he formulated his whole characteristic 'class' terminology: 'bourgeois', 'proletariat', and 'class' itself. As regards 'bourgeois', we can distinguish two aspects of the concept. There is 'bourgeois' as a fiction or tool of analysis, made necessary by that other fiction, 'the proletariat'. They are fictions in the sense of being working assumptions, according to which any situation of conflict can be analysed in terms of bourgeois versus proletariat, and from this point of view everyone on the ruling or exploiting side, whether he be landowner, manufacturer, banker, professor, etc., belongs to the 'bourgeoisie'. Secondly there is 'bourgeois' or 'bourgeoisie' as a slur, i.e. as an opprobrious name bestowed on a certain set of people supposed actually to exist and which, by dint of the 'species-fallacy', can be regarded as a recognizable human type.

Here we need to consider the whole matter of slurs. They function by means of a particular kind of prevarication, a trick of not letting it be known whether one is referring to the factual or the evaluative. 'Jew' or 'Jewish' is perhaps the most notorious of all slurs; and this slur works because there is (it cannot be denied) something you can objectively identify on racial or religious grounds as Jewishness. Thus the anti-Semite, when using 'Jewish' as a slur, can, if challenged, always pretend he was only referring to objective and neutral fact and was making no ethical imputation. He may even go over to the offensive and say: 'Are you suggesting that there is no such thing as a Jew?'

It is the same with 'bourgeois'. Marx could claim plausibly, because of the existence and popularity of this once legally descriptive word 'bourgeois', that the thing called the 'bourgeoisie' must exist—from which it is only a short step to say it has always existed. It is thus open to him to use 'bourgeois' as a purely ethical accusation—as you might say that someone is a 'hypocrite' or a 'miser'—yet to pass it off as a factual judgement. This is a basic rhetorical ploy, similar to the ploy by which in aristocratic societies, words like 'gentle' or 'base' are deliberately ambiguous, leaving it to the listener to decide whether they refer to ethical qualities or to social position.

For Marx 'bourgeois' became an all-purpose word of abuse. Karl Schurz, who knew him in the late 1840s, wrote in his *Reminiscences*:

I remember most distinctly the cutting disdain with which he pronounced the word *bourgeois*: and as a bourgeois—that is, as a detestable example of the deepest mental and moral degeneracy—he denounced everyone who dared oppose his opinions.[13]

I think, though, that behind this usage of Marx's there lurked a term more familiar to him and his friends in early years, that of 'Philistine', a term or war-cry indispensable to Heine and the Young Germans and before them to Goethe and the writers of the *Sturm und Drang*. It is an interesting term (akin to 'snob', in that it too was, by origin, university slang for an outsider or 'townee'), and Marx reverted to it throughout his life, in his less dogmatic moments. Rather touchingly, he invokes it in 1860 when trying to mend a quarrel with his old friend Freiligrath:

I tell you frankly that I cannot decide to let irrelevant misunderstandings lose me one of the few men whom I have loved as a friend in the eminent sense of the word . . . We both know that each of us in his own way, putting aside all private interest from the purest motives, has held aloft for years over the heads of the philistines the banner of the *classe la plus laborieuse et la plus misérable*.[14]

I bring the term in here because it helps us perceive the nature of a slur. 'Philistine' is not, in my sense, a slur, since, however fairly or unfairly it is applied, it plays no such trick as those more devious words 'bourgeois', 'class' etc.; it is simply and undisguisedly an ethical judgement.

Let us now turn to Flaubert. I choose him as the representative of a phenomenon profoundly important to French intellectual life. For Flaubert, as for Gide, for Sartre and for Roland Barthes, 'death to the bourgeois' is their new version of *écrasez l'infâme* and is the very mainspring of their spiritual life. I toy with the idea that this was the true French Romantic movement. In Britain, Romanticism was a profound and permanent revolution, and to a considerable extent we still think in categories supplied by Blake and Wordsworth. In France, by contrast, Romanticism was a mere 'movement', a movement in the arts, and perhaps not quite first-rate. French Romanticism, you might say, was not quite 'serious'; to *épater les bourgeois* by means of red waistcoats, untrimmed beards, and enjambed verses was part of a most invigorating game, played by very young men. 'It took all Victor Hugo's Olympic majesty and the shudders of terror he inspired', wrote Gautier in his *History of Romanticism* (1872),

to carry off his small turned-down collar—a concession to M. Prud-homme—and when the doors were closed, and no profane ones were present, this weakness of the great genius, which connected him with humanity and even with the *bourgeoisie*, was commented on sadly, and deep sighs welled up from our artistic breasts.

Gautier's tone, and his phrase 'connected him with humanity', are to the point. The infinitely stupid, petty-minded 'bourgeois', ritually slaughtered ten times a day by the Hugo circle, was a necessary fiction, projected by young men who, for the moment, had no wish to be 'connected with humanity'.*

* Some, of course, clung to the fiction for a lifetime. Gautier writes rather touchingly of meeting the poet 'Philothée O'Neddy', now middle-aged and quite forgotten, at a reunion of the Hugo circle many years later. ' "Well," said I, going up to him and shaking his hand. "When will your second volume of verse appear?" He gazed at me with his watery, frightened blue eyes, and answered with a sigh: "When there are no more bourgeois." '

It was another matter with Flaubert, who inherited this anti-
bourgeois mythology from the Romantics but with whom it took a
quite different and more serious development. The difference, I
should remark, was not a question of definitions. Flaubert when
flaying the 'bourgeois' was as carefree about sociological fact as
Philothée O'Neddy or the young Gautier. He was quite ready to see
the 'bourgeois' through the eyes of Molière and the *ancien régime*.
'Where has the Bourgeois loomed more gigantic than today?,' he
writes to Louis Bouilhet in 1850. 'What is Molière's in comparison?
M. Jourdain hardly rises to the knees of the first *négocien* [*sic*] you
meet in the street.'[15] And those who claim for Flaubert that he confirms Marx's judgements on nineteenth-century society have a problem in that one of Flaubert's favourite emblems for the 'bourgeoisie'
is the *grocer*—hardly a very 'Industrial-Revolution' or 'capitalist'
figure. I am not suggesting any absurdity in comparing Marx with
Flaubert, who, in his *Éducation sentimentale*, proved himself in some
ways a more advanced historian than professional-historian contemporaries. What I mean is that when he uses the word 'bourgeois' (as
when he sadly asks his close friend Alfred le Poittevin, who is getting
married: 'Are you sure, O great man, that you will not end up
becoming bourgeois?'[16]), he is not asking a sociological question.

The truth is, people do not easily give up a well-established slur.
It is too great a luxury, and they will perpetuate the slur, even where
the circumstances of its origin have changed beyond recognition. (A
hideous example of this is anti-Semitism.) In the reign of Louis XIV
there was invented on the part of the nobility a social slur upon the
bourgeoisie, and neither Marx nor Flaubert have any compunction
in perpetuating it.

So, to return to the Romantics: the essential difference between
them and Flaubert is that Flaubert *interiorized* the 'bourgeois' issue.
Why he has to assail and vilify all things 'bourgeois' is, as he real-
izes, because they are to be found in his own breast. They represent
vices belonging to the moral order, from which nobody can be sure
that he or she is free. The anti-'bourgeois' war is a form of quasi-
religious asceticism; and as such, there is no obvious end to it.

I will enumerate one or two of the issues or antitheses upon which
Flaubert's life turned. He was determined to realize and fulfil himself utterly, at least by the way of dreams; and on the other hand he
was, in his own view, not born to *enjoy*. He had a passionate craving
for riches and luxury, but a total contempt for all the ways he might
obtain them. He was resolved to understand everything, and this

seemed, for him, to demand *detachment* from everything—a detachment so complete that the most everyday matters and most banal phrases would 'grip him with amazement'. Thus he could take no practical interest in political or social reform and had comical hankerings after ancient tyranny, yet he became the laborious historian of the 1848 Revolution. Finally, he was possessed always with mad yearnings for escape ('Ah! the desert! the desert! a Turkish saddle! A mountain pass and an eagle calling from a cloud . . . '[17]); yet knew he would be lost without his 'corner of earth', his sublimely stupid and familiar Rouen.* For a name for a life constructed upon these antitheses, we need look no further than 'asceticism'. His self-identification with St Anthony was perfectly genuine; and rarely has asceticism been so fruitful.

Now the notion of the 'bourgeois' is central to this scheme of life. When Flaubert writes to Alfred de Poittevin 'The bourgeois . . . is for me something infinite' we can read the word 'infinite' as 'inexhaustible'. The 'bourgeois' is the most convenient name for the eternal enemy inside himself which, in St Anthony-like fashion, it is his life-task to combat. It stands, first of all, for the interested (the gainful, the utilitarian) as against the disinterested; it stands for brute matter as against ideas, the *idée reçue* against originality, the mechanical against the spontaneous, the fallacy of possessions and possession as against the truths of contemplation and imagination. And these are all temptations which are not conquered once and for all but have to be combated day after day. It is a commonplace of literary history, but a crucially important fact, that Flaubert could create Emma Bovary and Bouvard and Pécuchet because he *was* them, they were merely transpositions of his own temptations. This is no pat diagnosis in Flaubert's case; it was a truth he had to re-learn, and it went with generosity of feeling. It is impressive to see how the further he progressed in writing those novels, the more his sympathies went out to and embraced his absurd heroes and heroines.

* 'Have you sometimes seen, while walking on the cliffs, a slender and wayward plant, hanging from the crest of a rock and spreading its waving locks over the abyss below? The wind shook it, trying to dislodge it, and as for the plant—it stretched outwards into the air as if to escape with it. Only a single unseen root nailed it to the stone, whilst its being seemed to dilate, to irradiate into the surroundings, wanting to take flight. Well, say the day comes when a stronger wind uproots it, what will happen to it? The sun will parch it on the sand, the rain will rot it to shreds. I too am attached to a corner of the earth . . . '

(Letter to Louise Colet, 29 Aug. 1847)

Flaubert's notion of the 'bourgeois' and of the war with the 'bourgeois' has been a dominating one for intellectuals throughout the succeeding century. Thomas Mann once said that all his own work could be understood as effort to free himself from the bourgeoisie,[18] and I think we are to take this in the Flaubertian sense, i.e. that he did not expect to *succeed* in this, nor would it make much sense to talk of succeeding. We may compare what W. H. Auden wrote very perceptively in an article, 'Authority in America':

Looking back it seems to me that the interest in Marx taken by myself and my friends . . . was more psychological than political; we were interested in Marx in the same way that we were interested in Freud, as a technique of unmasking middle class ideologies, not with the intention of repudiating our class, but with the hope of becoming better bourgeois.[19]

Taken in this quasi-religious—self-improving and self-mortifying—sense, the 'war with the bourgeois' is a respect-worthy and potentially grand enterprise. It is true that Sartre, in his vast unfinished study of Flaubert, *L'Idiot de la famille*, sees in it no more than bad faith, and precisely because it is non-political and merely a quest for personal salvation. Flaubert, according to Sartre, does not want the 'bourgeoisie' to disappear, indeed he is very anxious that it should remain; he merely wants not to be *of* it.

If he claimed to be disembourgeoising himself, it was to be by his own private efforts, a matter of a solitary and meritorious conversion, and on condition that the bourgeois class should remain intact, both outside himself and even *inside*—a Promethean vulture gnawing his liver, simultaneously increasing his personal merit and relieving him from material cares.[20]

Against this, one has to set one's feeling that Sartre's way of talking about 'class' in *L'Idiot de la famille* is desperately sliding and inconsistent. At some moments his bourgeois is almost comically flesh-and-blood—rich, ruthless and exploitative, yet too stupid to invent his own ideology; at others his 'bourgeoisie' grows quite shadowy and disintegrates into a medley of arbitrary groupings: *nantis* ('the fully provided-for'), *demi-nantis* ('the semi-provided-for'), and *classes moyennes* which stretch, in *couches* ('layers'), from the *demi-nantis* down to shopkeepers.[21] (A similar slither, of course, often bothers us in Marx.)

What the case of Flaubert brings home to us is that 'bourgeois' is not always and necessarily a 'class' term. It is significant that we feel no compulsion to nag Flaubert with the 'belonging' question ('if you are not to belong to the bourgeoisie, where *are* you to belong?').

There is another kind of success at which, in his 'war with the bourgeois', Flaubert seems dimly to be aiming, and this is not to escape
from the bourgeoisie (which is hardly a possibility, even logically),
but to escape from 'class' and 'class' thinking in general. For if the
'war with the bourgeois' were to become *wholly* interiorized and
purely a conflict within the individual soul, all connection would be
severed between it and 'class'.

3

Marx's unwritten chapter

I come now to the first and greatest theorist of 'class': Karl Marx. As is well known, in volume 3 of *Capital* there was to have been a chapter on 'Classes', but Marx only managed to write a few opening sentences—for which the reason may not only have been his death. Thus we have to piece together his theory of 'class' from his other many scattered remarks and discussions. Luckily, though, this task has been made easier for us by Ralf Dahrendorf who, in his *Class and Class Conflict in Industrial Society* (1959), has boldly written Marx's chapter for him. My own brief outline of Marx's theory will lean heavily on Dahrendorf.

Here, then, is how I understand Marx's theory. 'Classes' are to be defined, or they define themselves, by reference not to source of income (for in that case doctors or civil servants or fishermen would be 'classes');[1] nor to relative size of purse; but to role in the productive process (i.e. to those 'concrete relationships' of domination and subjection which obtain in the sphere of production). There are two *political* classes, and two only, the proletariat and the bourgeoisie. It is their struggle which is 'the great lever of social change'.[2] And these two political classes draw their membership from the 'three great *social* (*gesellschaftlichen*) classes of modern society based on a capitalist mode of production',[3] viz., wage-labourers, industrialists and landowners. (Industrialists and landowners form 'the two great interests into which the *bourgeoisie* is split'.)[4] There are, indeed, other 'classes' (whether we are to consider them as political or social). For instance the middle estates (*Mittelstände*, small manufacturers, small shopkeepers, artisans, peasants, and the *Lumpenproletariat*;[5] but these can on a long-term view be disregarded, since capitalist society is increasingly polarizing itself into a stark opposition of bourgeois and proletariat.

The concept of 'classes' is required, specifically, to explain social conflict. 'The history of all hitherto existing society is the history of class struggles.'[6] Moreover a society based on class conflict requires an oppressed class as a condition of its existence; from which it follows that 'the condition for the emancipation of the working class' is 'the abolition of all classes'.[7] Thus a 'class' is by definition a conflict-group. 'The separate individuals form a class only in so far as they have to carry on a common battle against another class.'[8] On the other hand, the members of a class can be in a state of conflict with those of another class without being aware of the fact. What is at stake, rather, is an objective conflict of *interests*.

It is not a question of what this or that proletarian or even the whole prolet ariat, at the moment *regards* as its aim. It is a question of what the proletariat is, and what, in accordance with this being, it will be historically compelled to do. Its aim and historical action is visibly and irrevocably foreshadowed in its own life situation as well as in the whole organisation of bourgeois society today.[9]

So much for my summary. What, of course, one needs above all to remember about Marx's theory of 'class' is that it is, as Dahrendorf rightly insists, a 'heuristic' concept. It is a logical instrument, a tool for the explanation of social change. It is not, that is to say, intended to be descriptive; we are not supposed to look round and expect to find, visibly and in flesh-and-blood before us, a 'bourgeoisie' or a 'proletariat' any more than Economic Man is to be met with in the street or is listed in the telephone book.

It will be seen, though, that Marx's theory of 'class' has its elusive aspects—for instance as to the rules dictating when you are to picture two classes, or three classes, or an indefinite number. Again there is an awkwardness in a given set of people constituting a 'class' from a social point of view but not from a political (or politico-economic) one. Further, Marx, at first sight, vacillates on the matter of class-consciousness, i.e. whether a 'class' can be a 'class' without being aware of it. In *The Eighteenth Brumaire* he writes: 'In so far as there is merely a local interconnection among these small-holding peasants, and the identity of their interests begets no community, no national bond and no political organization among them, they do not form a class',[10] and this seems to contradict the quotation cited above ('It is not a question . . . '), which suggests that the consciousness of a 'class' is not of serious concern; what matters is its objective 'life situation'. In *The Poverty of Philosophy* he attempts, but not too convincingly, to bridge the two views by means of the Hegelian distinction between the 'in itself' (*an sich*) and the 'for itself' (*für sich*): 'The domination of capital had created for this mass [of workers] a common situation, common interests. This mass is thus already a class as against capital, but not yet for itself.'[11]

However it would be silly to approach Marx in a nitpicking spirit; and if it is true there are tangles in his theory of 'class', no doubt he might have straightened them out in his unwritten chapter. It is a quite different consideration which impresses me, and a more important one. It concerns Marx's use of the term 'bourgeois'. If all Marx wanted from the concepts of 'class' and of 'bourgeois' versus 'proletariat' was a 'heuristic' and analytical tool, you would have expected him to try to purge the word 'bourgeois' of its historical associations. But on the contrary he insists on them, and with dizzying effect. The 'modern bourgeoisie', if we are to believe the *Communist Manifesto*, is inheritor of all the older bourgeoisies:

An oppressed class under the sway of the feudal nobility, an armed and self-governing association in the medieval commune; here independent urban republic (as in Italy and Germany), there taxable 'third estate' of the monarchy (as in France); afterwards, in the period of manufacture proper, serving either the semi-feudal or the absolute monarchy as a counterpoise against the nobility, and, in fact, corner-stone of the great monarchies in general, the bourgeoisie has at last, since the establishment of modern industry and of the world market, conquered for itself, in the modern parliamentary State, exclusive political sway. The executive of the modern State is but a committee for managing the common affairs of the whole bourgeoisie.[12]

Through all its history, he says, it has been a force for progress, the evil and Nibelung-like agent of a beneficent change—beneficent because it has faced mankind with reality, which is a necessary prelude to further change.

The bourgeoisie, historically, has played a 'most revolutionary' part:

wherever it has got the upper hand, [it] has put an end to all feudal, patriarchal, idyllic relations. It has pitilessly torn asunder the motley feudal ties that bound man to his 'natural superiors', and has left no other nexus between man and man than naked self-interest, than callous 'cash payment'. It has drowned the most heavenly ecstasies of religious fervour, of chivalrous enthusiasm, of philistine sentimentalism, in the icy waters of egotistical calculation. It has resolved personal worth in exchange value and in place of the numberless indefeasible chartered freedoms has set up that single, unconscionable freedom—Free Trade. In one word, for exploitation veiled by religious and political illusion it has substituted naked, shameless, direct, brutal exploitation.[13]

Marx's phrase 'wherever it has got the upper hand' must mean that the 'bourgeoisie' has always, potentially or at bottom, been the same entity—a similar ruthless set of people, Gradgrinds and Mr

Moneybagses with no thought in their head but the cash nexus. Hence, so far as they are concerned, what is new in the nineteenth-century situation is merely their final triumph and doffing of the mask. They have not changed, only revealed themselves, under the favourable conditions of the Industrial Revolution. And if the landed gentry are now to be lumped under the same name ('bourgeoisie') it is not because the landed gentry have ceased to be prominent and influential (for plainly they have not), but because they, on the other hand, *have* changed and have become, not parfit gentil knights but Gradgrinds too.

Now if *The Communist Manifesto* were meant to be taken literally, objections would come crowding in: among them, that we had supposed the 'bourgeois' or burgesses, in the past, to have been famous *champions* of 'indefeasible chartered freedoms' (what else are 'freedoms of the city'?). The dialectic can do much, but some paradoxes even the dialectic cannot encompass. But then I don't suggest Marx meant such things or could have held such a caricatural view of history. It is just that if you start picturing the 'bourgeoisie' and the 'proletariat' as sets of real people, and not just as a heuristic fiction, you are doomed to land up in farce.

Consider, as another scene of farce, the foreign visitor learning that the English for 'bourgeois' is 'middle class' and drawing his conclusions about the 'middle class' from the study of dukes. The dukes are naturally amazed. Have they not been brought up, in their innocence, to think that their 'class'-position turns primarily upon their *not* being 'middle class'? (As we know, the Cecil family had a not very attractive family joke about 'MCMs' or 'Middle-class Monsters'.) Now here, you may say, is a beautiful exploit on Marx's part, to have so disrespectfully incorporated English aristocrats into the 'bourgeoisie'. And, indeed, that the nineteenth-century landed gentry in Britain were very different from their ancestors, much more different than they would have liked to think—that there was sham-medievalism in their self-image as well as in their houses—we can assent to gleefully. So if, more generally, Marxist theory is going to discredit and explode the 'class'-theories of Victorian Britons, and what you might call 'innocent' class-theory in general, it may be just what was needed. However, when we find Marx actually performing this outflanking manœuvre, for instance in an article 'Tories and Whigs' in the *New York Daily Tribune*, we sense at once that it is no *more* than a satirical manœuvre. He writes:

The year 1846 transformed the Tories into Protectionists. Tory was the sacred name, Protectionist is the profane one; Tory was the political battle-cry, Protectionist is the economical shout of distress; Tory seemed an idea, a principle, Protectionist is an interest. Protectionists of what? Of their own revenues, of the rent of their own land. Then the Tories, in the end, are bourgeois as much as the remainder, for where is the bourgeois who is not a protectionist of his own purse?[14]

Plainly this *tu quoque* or 'And you're another' ploy is purely rhetorical and is not being offered as serious analysis.

Something else strikes us here, of a more general nature. As I have said earlier, it is impossible to use the terms 'middle class' or 'upper class' or 'working class' without mentally assigning oneself to a 'class', or at least to a set of feelings (proud or anxious or derisive as the case may be) about one's own 'class'-position; it is in this manner that the words function. But then, it seems plain that the users of the terms 'bourgeois' and 'proletariat' in their Marxist sense also feel that, in so doing, they speak as members of a class-system. However, with them matters work rather differently, for it usually goes with their wishing rather passionately that they were *not*. It has been the occupational hazard or even mania of intellectuals, from Flaubert onwards, to feel deep guilt at belonging to the 'bourgeoisie' and to be always striving to purge and exorcise the 'bourgeois' in themselves. As we saw with Flaubert, there is something admirable and honourable in this. If you regard 'classes' simply as conflict-groups, it is what conscience would dictate, for the alternative to belonging to the 'proletariat' must be to be its enemy. However, what this heart-searching by intellectuals proves is that, after all, they are still partly thinking of 'classes' in a naïve pre-Marxist way. It suggests that they believe they can actually detach themselves from the 'class-system' altogether, though strict Marxist theory would condemn this as Utopian fantasy.

There is a striking example of this in Roland Barthes. In the final section of his *Mythologies* (1957), under the title 'Myth Today', he theorizes about his role as 'mythologue', or professional demystifier of 'bourgeois' mythology and ideology; and every sentence seems to assume that neither he nor his readers belong to the 'bourgeoisie' themselves—though, as I have said, the only alternative would seem to be to belong to the 'proletariat', which he pretty plainly is not claiming for himself (and, however we juggle with words, would be preposterous). There is a paradox here, an illogical claim to privileged and neutral status, of a kind my reader is by now familiar with.

It is a paradox which, indirectly, Barthes faces in the same essay—a very brilliant and heartfelt one. The neo-Marxist 'mythologue' like himself, he says, condemns himself to loneliness and dispossession. To expose the mythology of 'good French wine', as he does in his essay 'Wine and Milk', is at the same time to cut himself off from the myth-consumers—i.e. the people who also actually enjoy the wine; for after all wine is objectively good. The mythologue, in fact, is cutting himself off from humanity in general, so that his remaining connection with the human world is 'of the order of sarcasm'.

One must go even further; in a sense, the mythologue is excluded from the history in the name of which he professes to act . . . The mythologue is not even in a Moses-like situation: he cannot see the Promised Land. For him, tomorrow's positivity is entirely hidden by today's negativity.

Let us look a little more at the origins of Marx's thought on 'class'. It is instructive, and even exciting, to observe the birth of Marx's actual terminology of 'class'. One can date the birth fairly exactly, to the last months of 1843. So far as the word 'class' (*Klasse*) itself is concerned, it is a matter of this word supplanting the word 'estate' (*Stand*); and this was no pedantic nicety, but a far-reaching event. During the spring and summer of 1843 Marx had employed himself in writing a lengthy *Contribution to the Critique of Hegel's 'Philosophy of Law'*. Hegel, in his *Philosophie des Rechts*[15] (1821), had constructed a philosophical rationale for a society based, in 'medieval' style, on 'estates'. According to his scheme, Reason and the nature of things assigned individuals to one or other of three 'estates' (*Stände*), viz.: the 'substantial' (or agricultural) estate; the 'reflecting or formal' (i.e. business) estate; and the 'universal' (or bureaucratic) estate—so called because its members would be paid to devote themselves not to a sectional interest, but to the interests of the State as a whole. Hegel's State was to be an organism in which the institutions of civil life (corporations, associations, and craft-fellowships, etc.) would be in a harmonic or organic relationship to the institutions of political life, and in which the connection between the 'estates' of civil life and the 'Estates' of parliament should be a substantial, not just a verbal, one.

Marx of course makes a wholesale onslaught on this, the gist of his attack being that the scheme, drawn out in such masterly fashion by Hegel, presents an absolutely accurate account of things as they are in Prussia and for this very reason is a most devastating *exposé*. It depicts a mode of life in which civil society, cut off from true political life, grows utterly spiritless and dead, and in which Man's 'species-being' is denied. Marx here writes as a committed humanist.*

---

* Marx's concern for Man's 'species-being' seems a strong argument against those, like Althusser, who would reject the description of him as a 'humanist'. But see p.49.

Throughout his critique, Marx goes along with Hegel's actual term, *Stand* ('estate')—a term which was (and to some degree still is*) the accepted one for such social groupings in Germany and implies the existence of an 'organic' and ordered society. ('Estate' is here not far in meaning from 'calling'.) Significantly, Hegel himself occasionally applies the word *Klasse* to a social grouping, and precisely when he is depicting the ills that arise when humans are not organized in 'estates'. For instance, he writes about the *nouveaux riches*:

> when complaints are made about the luxury of the business *classes* [my italics] and their passion for extravagance—which have as their concomitant the creation of a rabble of paupers—we must not forget that besides its other causes (e.g. increasing mechanisation of labour) this phenomenon has an ethical ground . . . Unless he is a member of an authorised Corporation . . . an individual is without rank or dignity, his isolation reduces his business to mere self-seeking . . . Consequently he has to try to gain recognition for himself by giving external proofs of success in his business . . . He cannot live in the manner of his *estate*, for no estate really exists for him . . . [16]

For the moment, Marx does not take up the offered word *Klasse* (class), so important to him later. On the other hand, by a play on words, he contrives at one point to turn Hegel's word 'estate' against him. Civil society divorced from political life, he says, is a formless and meaningless affair. Only one thing is characteristic about it, namely: 'that lack of property and the estate of direct labour, of concrete labour, form not so much an estate of civil society as the ground upon which its circles rest and move'. He is here obliquely, and without using the actual words, invoking a propertyless 'working class' or 'proletariat', and, so it seems to me, making a sort of sardonic pun on *Stand* (a word closely allied to the English 'stand'). His meaning is something like: 'It is not so much that propertyless workers are a *Stand* as that everyone else *stands* on them.'

Soon after the writing of his *Critique* Marx moved to Paris, to work with Ruge on the newly founded *Deutsch-französische Jahrbücher*. It was a crucial moment in his development. He was immediately in the thick of socialist activity, Fourierist and Proudhonist, and he visited all the various workers' associations, both *émigré* German and French, conceiving an intense admiration for their spirit. Soon, some

---

* Ralf Dahrendorf writes: 'It is significant that in conversational German the word 'class' is even today confined to the two strata of entrepreneurs and workers. Neither the nobility nor the professions nor the older groups of craftsmen and peasants are called classes. They are 'estates'—a concept which in the case of the 'middle estate' (*Mittelstand*) has been retained even for the newer groups of white-collar workers and civil servants' (*Class and Class Conflict in Industrial Society* (1959), pp. 6–7).

five months after the writing of his *Critique* of Hegel, he composed an 'Introduction' to a projected revision of it, in which the characteristic Marxian 'class' terminology—*Klasse, bourgeois* and *proletariat*—appears complete and in full working order. *Klasse* would be a natural suggestion from the French *classe* of Louis Blanc and others. *Bourgeois* he is employing in a usage deriving from Saint-Simon (and he will always use this French word in preference to its German equivalent *bürgerlich*, which means merely 'civil' or 'civic'). And *Proletarier* (proletarian) and *Proletariat* were very recent introductions into German from French, again under Saint-Simonian influence,[17] the adjective *prolétaire* being a long-established part of French vocabulary but the noun *prolétariat* being, even in French, a neologism of the 1830s and initially not the name of a social class but an abstract noun meaning 'indigence' or 'destitution'. (The word is still in transition in the early Proudhon.)

This 'Introduction', published in the first and only (double) number of the ill-fated *Deutsch-französische Jahrbücher*, was one of Marx's most dazzling and innovatory writings. Its theme is that the only possible salvation for Germany, and if for Germany then for the world, lies: 'in the formation of a class with radical chains,* a class of civil society which is not a class of civil society, an estate which is the dissolution of all estates, a sphere which has a universal character by its universal suffering and claims no *particular right* because no *particular wrong* but wrong generally is perpetrated against it; which can no longer invoke a *historical* but only a *human* title . . . '. This 'sphere' of society can only emancipate itself by emancipating itself from all other spheres of society, thereby emancipating all those other spheres also. It is (a quintessentially Marxist) turn of thought at one and the same time a group of men and 'the complete loss of man', only able to win itself through the complete re-winning of man. It not merely reflects, but actually 'is' the dissolution of the 'estate' idea. And its name is *the proletariat*. 'This dissolution of society as a particular estate is the *proletariat*.'

Much of the force and drama of this manifesto (a precursor to the *Communist Manifesto* of 1848) lies in *naming*. Its evocation of a class characterized by '*universal*' suffering' is a deliberate allusion to, and ironic turning on the head of, Hegel's '*universal* estate' of bureaucrats. And the whole argument turns on the rejection of the term

---

* 'Radikalen Ketten'. This rather obscure expression seems from the context to mean something like 'particularly onerous chains, binding it to the very roots of its being'.

'estate' (*Stand*), with its implications of social harmony, in favour of the indiscriminate and 'alienating' term 'class' (*Klasse*). (It seems strange that the standard modern translations, by J. O'Malley, of Marx's *Critique* and its 'Introduction',[18] render *Stand*, as often as not, by 'class', thus quite blunting Marx's meaning.)

Marx's theory of 'class', as will be seen, is remote from, and deliberately at odds with, what you might call 'purely social' or 'innocent' class-theory, with its concern for 'class-distinctions', class-shibboleths etc. A Marxist has to dismiss 'innocent' class-notions as irrelevant—irrelevant, I mean, to the theory of 'class', though of course they may have significance as a symptom. Now this setting-up of a true Marxist-historical account of 'class', in which class-conflict is the prime mover in history at all periods, against the false and trivial, though symptomatic, talk about 'class' in a purely 'social' sense, which came in after 1815, is a pretty bold gesture. And if Marx were going to make it, he would, you feel, need to hold to it very rigidly and consider it a point of honour not to let 'innocent' notions infect the informed judgement of historical materialism. But as it turns out, he is far from rigid; on the contrary he mixes up the two flagrantly and unrepentantly whenever it happens to suit him. And what this suggests is that, remote as 'innocent' theory and Marxist theory are, they are alike in one respect, they are both of them essentially transactional—their mode of employment is strategic and concerned with the securing of certain political or social ends.

As I said earlier, it is plain that in Marx's class-theory desire is furiously at work—namely, the desire that there *should* be 'classes' and 'class-conflict' and a successful proletarian revolution. What, in that first dramatic announcement of 'class', Marx is proclaiming is not so much the existence of the proletariat as the need to create one. His wording: 'the formation of a class with radical chains, a class of civil society which is not a class of civil society', etc. is equivocal, and what this equivocation allows for is the fatal element in Marxism: its disingenuous dealings with 'consciousness'.

There is, one cannot help thinking, something vicious in that whole Marxist-style notion of 'proletarian consciousness' or 'revolutionary consciousness', wherein 'consciousness' figures as something less or more than, or anyway something different from, 'thought'. As a mode of argument it embraces all possible contradictions. At one moment it is said: the supreme need is that workers should acquire revolutionary consciousness, or have it instilled into them; at another, that the workers may not actually acquire true revolutionary consciousness till after the Revolution has happened—it will be the fruit, not the cause, of revolution; at another again that it doesn't matter if they have revolutionary consciousness or not, since it is not what they think and feel that counts, but their life-situation objectively considered. The doctrine of 'consciousness' has always a taint of prevarication; and the roots of this lie, as we can perceive, in the German-philosopher mode of thought of Marx's 'Introduction' to the *Critique of Hegel*—the brilliant and paradox-juggling style according to which the proletariat may 'be' the 'dissolution of society as a particular estate' (or again, Germany may 'be' the 'deficiency of the political present constituted as a particular world').[19] What the style conceals is a human impossibility. Some have compared the redemptive role allotted by Marx to the 'proletariat' to that of Christ the 'Man of Sorrows'. But if Marx's words are to be taken literally, he would be asking more of the worker than was asked of Christ, in fact something impossible to ask—i.e. for the worker to sacrifice everything whatever, including his very *humanity*, on behalf of some unspecified future generation. It is in order not to be proposing this as a real-life dialogue, such as might plausibly be held between an individual intellectual and an individual worker, that Marx has to invoke the concept of 'consciousness'—being neither exactly thought, nor feeling, nor conviction, nor even, necessarily, conscious. One reflects that novelists, like Tolstoy or George Eliot, needing to flesh out their ideas in human form, would have been less likely to fall into this error.

Nor are we to consider it as unimportant, a mere quibble over definitions and semantics, that there should be this prevarication in Marx's thought, and that he should save the definition 'proletariat' by an equivocation over 'consciousness'. It is just here that he gives warrant to Lenin, a thinker of a very different spirit (and one whom nobody would ever accuse of 'humanism'). Definitions and semantics take the stage momentously in the October Revolution, and the most horrifying moment in the Revolution comes—surely?—when the Cheka are ordered to go out and arrest the 'bourgeois'. 'We are exterminating the bourgeoisie as a class,' writes the Cheka chief Latsis:

Don't look for evidence or proof showing that this or that person either by word or deed acted against the interests of the Soviet power. The first question you should put to the arrested person is: To what class does he belong, what is his origin, what was his education, and what is his profession? These should determine the fate of the accused. This is the essence of the Red Terror.[20]

It is hard, after this episode, not to react with a shudder to the whole concept of 'class'.

4

'Class' and the historians

I come next to the attitude of twentieth-century historians towards 'class' terminology—towards terms like 'upper class' and 'middle class', 'bourgeois' and 'proletarian'. Their attitude seems often to have been one of worry or exasperation. I think for instance of Alfred Cobban, who wrote with sarcasm about that epithet 'bourgeois', affixed so successfully by the Saint-Simonians to the July Revolution and July Monarchy.

everyone knows that the régime of Louis-Philippe in France represented the rule of the *bourgeoisie*. Because everyone knows this, nobody troubles to see if it is correct. Yet what are the facts? The franchise was based on the payment of direct taxes, which were imposed mostly on the land. It has been shown that between 82 and 90 per cent of the electorate derived the income by which it secured the vote from the land. Five to 9 per cent from commerce, 2 to 5 per cent from industry, and 2 to 4 per cent from the liberal professions. Louis-Philippe had in all 60 ministers in the course of his reign. Of these, 8 were aristocrats, 36 civil or military officials, 9 lawyers and professors, and 7 representatives of trade, industry and finance.[1]

Cobban comments drily: 'Such facts suggest that the "bourgeois monarchy" deserves a little more investigation before we can take it for granted.' Or again, Shirley Gruner, whom the problems in defining 'bourgeois' lead at last—as definition-problems tend to do, with social historians—to a despairing or draconian conclusion:

the expression *bourgeoisie* does not in itself refer to any unambiguous category, such as, for instance, 'university professors'. In the everyday sense the word is about as vague as such notions as power, force and energy before their definition by science. To achieve unambiguity, it must be defined in some way. What is most definitely impermissible is to project one's own presumed definition into the realm of reality and treat it as one of the 'facts' of history. With this 'fallacy of misplaced concreteness', many strange results can be obtained. After all, the 'bourgeoisie' is not something to touch or examine in the same way as a stone or a beetle. It is a concept, part of a general network of ideas set up to arrange, stratify, and categorise levels of social existence. Of course, this presupposes a generally accepted definition but, as we have seen, the word 'bourgeoisie' has never had the good fortune to be defined in any one strict sense . . . In view of this would it not be preferable to abandon it? This might appear a drastic step but the word is so involved with the rationalistic theories of the early nineteenth century and their emotional conflicts that it might make for clearer thinking if a new term were introduced.[2]

Now these complaints of Cobban and Gruner prompt me to a rather large objection. Do they not imply that social terms like 'bourgeois' exist mainly for the benefit of historians? Ordinary people (among whom we must include, perhaps, Saint-Simon and Marx, as well as Molière and those rude court-pages in Sorel's *Francion*) are not to be trusted with the word. They have been so irresponsible, have so blunted the edge of this precious tool of the historian, that it is no longer fit for serious use, and he will have to procure himself a new one. So the argument seems to run; and it assumes that the historian needs such a tool, or could employ it if he had it. Well, as I have said earlier, I would contest this. In the world at large, under the impulsion of various desires and purposes, people have categorized one another, and by corollary themselves, 'socially' in a variety of ways—and these ways it is imperative for the historian to investigate. But this need not mean the historian should, as it were, go out into the streets or the *salons* and imitate those of whom he writes. Just because a nineteenth-century person asserts the existence of a 'class', a historian does not have to go along with him or her, indeed one would expect him to be chary of doing so; for by so doing he would in a sense be handing over his duties as historian to the nineteenth-century person.

After all, 'the middle class' is not a thing but a concept, and a distinctly tendentious concept, involving a judgement of value, viz., that some people are socially 'higher' and 'in the middle' and 'lower'. It is in this respect a concept like 'the True Church' or 'pure English', and a historian needs to think twice or thrice before adopting it as a description of 'reality'. Social historians, like others, seem to agree that 'class' concepts are remarkably troublesome and sometimes grow quite anguished over the problem of how to define them, or indignant at others for their carelessness in defining them. But is not much of the trouble self-made and a result of looking for the wrong thing—of assuming wrongly that there can be a purified and redeemed terminology of 'class' available for use by experts? The truth is that in studying the concept of 'social class' one is, or should be, studying one thing only, viz., the ways in which ordinary people apply, and have applied, social categories to themselves and others.

One often reads in historians the 'broad-minded' view that the way in which men and women in the past have pictured their own society is a matter of serious interest, not beneath the notice of a scholar. Here is Arlette Jouanna, in *Ordre social: mythes et hiérarchies dans la France du XVIᵉ siècle*:

One of the most challenging questions faced by a historian concerns the manner in which men in the past have represented to themselves the society in which they lived, how they saw its various elements and perceived the hierarchy ordering them. The answer to such a question is precious not merely because of the light it throws on modes of human thought (*mentalités*); it also illuminates social structures themselves, to the extent to which society and the image which individuals and groups form of that society influence each other and interpenetrate.[3]

My reaction to this is to say: in so far as you are studying concepts like 'orders', or 'ranks', or 'estates', or again the concept 'class', the 'answer to such a question' is not only 'precious', it is all you can ever be seeking. Needless to say, there are various other aspects—for instance the economic, or the political, or the demographic—from which you can study societies. But in so far as you are studying 'classes' or 'estates' or 'ranks' or 'orders' you cannot, having analysed the contemporary ideas about them in some society, then go on to explain what the truth of the matter 'really' was. This would be a delusion, for there is no reality of this kind.

It is this illusion which seems to be at work, in a particularly obvious way, when the historians Alan Everitt and Lawrence Stone try to give scientific definition to a category they call the 'pseudo-gentry': a group in late seventeenth-century and early Georgian England who were commonly regarded as gentry but, according to Stone and Everitt, were not 'really' gentry (because they didn't possess landed estates, or were down on their luck, or spent their time pursuing heiresses at Bath or Tunbridge Wells).[4] Now this is a kind of social judgement that dowagers and others were no doubt often making at the time, with significant shakings of the head, in the punp-room at Bath. But then, people would also have been passing such judgements in the Vicarage at Wakefield, and in the parlour of the 'Bell' at Edmonton, and it is exceedingly unlikely that all these judgements would have agreed. Can it be for the historian to come along two centuries later and settle such a matter for them? It seems, for a historian, a very unbecoming descent into the social arena.

A related problem arises when E. P. Thompson, in an article 'Eighteenth-century English society; class-struggle without class?',[5]

decides to refer to those who were not gentry in eighteenth-century
England as 'plebs'. He chooses the name, he explains, in preference
to 'working class' because in the eighteenth century 'many urban
artisans evinced the "vertical consciousness" of "the Trade" rather
than the "horizontal" consciousness of a mature industrial working
class'.[6] The attraction of the term 'plebs' for him is clearly that it
was used at the time, so that in some sense it cannot but embody historical reality. But the trouble with this lies in the further question,
who did the using? One cannot suppose that his 'plebs'—whoever
they include—would have referred to themselves as 'plebs' or
plebeians. The choice of names is a double bluff on Thompson's
part, and his heart is with the 'plebs'; nevertheless, my point is that
it aligns him inescapably with a ducal point of view.

One sometimes notices the same in other social historians: they
tend to talk as if they were dukes and only the ducal viewpoint had
'reality'. Brian Manning, in *The English People and the English Revolution* (1976), continually quotes spokesmen who allude to 'the
meaner sort of people', 'prentices and baser sorts of citizens', 'the
scum of all the profanest rout'; and somehow this language seems to
infect his own vision, so that when he has to sort out the inhabitants
of Birmingham in the 1640s, he categorizes them as 'the better sort
of people', 'the middle sort of people', and 'the inferior sort'. One
sees why he does it, it protects him from the accusation that he is
imposing modern categories; nevertheless it is at the cost of
impersonating a seventeenth-century grandee. How did the 'inferior
sort' draw the social lines, we wonder? Without doubt very differently, very likely not in three categories but in some other number;
and pretty certainly so as to distinguish themselves also from some
'inferior sort'. Why should their social vision have less truth-value
than the other, or than the various other ones?

Or shall we think for a moment of R. S. Neale and the 'Five-class
Model'[7] which he offers for the analysis of English society in the
1820s. Here is the model:

1 *Upper class*, aristocratic, landholding, authoritarian, exclusive.
2 *Middle class*, big industrial and commercial property-owners, senior
  military and professional men, aspiring to acceptance by the upper
  class, deferential towards the upper class because of this and because of
  concern for property and achieved position, but often individuated or
  privatized.
3 *Middling class*, petit bourgeois, aspiring professional men, other literates
  and artisans, individuated or privatized like the middle class but collec-

tively less deferential and more concerned to remove the privileges and authority of the upper class in which, without radical changes, they cannot realistically hope to share.

4 *Working class* A, industrial proletariat in factory areas, workers in domestic industries, collectivist and non-deferential and wanting government intervention to protect rather than liberate them.

5 *Working class* B, agricultural labourers, other low-paid non-factory urban labourers, domestic servants, urban poor, most working-class women whether from working-class A or B households, deferential and dependent.

This, as will be seen, employs terms ('Upper class', 'Middle class', 'Middling class', and 'Working class') used by people at the time, but not in the way that they used them: for the contemporaries of Cobbett had their own tripartite scheme, as opposed to this quintuple one, and they did not talk about 'Working class A' and 'Working class B'. Ancient mental arrangements have been razed, and a fine new steel and concrete building, with movable partitions, has been erected to house 'social classes' and 'political classes', 'strata' and 'quasi-groups'. (Though a few homely house-fronts have been allowed to remain, for the look of the thing.) However, a simple test will show that, purpose-built as it is, the building does not fulfil its purpose. If you try to accommodate the characters of *Middlemarch* in it, you find that hardly any will fit. Mr Brooke could just scrape in, through being a landowner, but you could not call that *fitting*. Casaubon does not fit, nor do the Vincys, nor does Lydgate. (For plainly some degree of coherence is being posited among the various categories within each group—otherwise why five groups and not twenty-five?—and whereas Lydgate is an 'aspiring professional man' he is in no sense 'petit bourgeois'.) It seems clear what has gone wrong. Neale has the notion that people can be categorized in an objective fashion, a fashion true for all possible observers. This must surely be an illusion? And even assuming it were true, the scheme involved could not take the form of a set of distinct compartments, whether three or five or a hundred; it would have, rather, to be a *moiré* design, a matter of numerous overlapping or interpenetrating patterns.

A more systematic example of the same illusion is to be found, or so it seems to me, in Pierre Goubert's *The Ancien Régime: French Society 1600–1750*.[8] In introducing a chapter on 'Bourgeois and Bourgeoisies', Goubert says he could restrict himself to a perfunctory and pigeon-holing definition of the *ancien régime* bourgeoisie, or alternatively he could embark, with the aid of a computer, on the systematic statistical study of the 'successive and simultaneous meanings' of the words bourgeois and bourgeoisie. However he will do neither. Instead:

We shall fall back upon a simple two-stage method: first, to grasp the *ancien régime* concept of 'bourgeois' by staying close to the documents; second, to attempt to elicit 'structures' by applying the by now almost commonplace formula of going from the 'lived' to the 'real'; in simpler terms, to develop our interpretation by drawing back the veil of appearance to restore the various bourgeois groups to their original place in the prevailing system—inside, occasionally on the fringes, and perhaps also outside it.

So the chapter falls into two halves. First we have 'The Contemporary View'—a very instructive exploration of what he enumerates as the 'good dozen current senses' of the terms 'bourgeois' and 'bourgeoisie' under the *ancien régime* ('general and emotive senses', 'juridical senses', and a 'narrow social sense'). Then we come to the 'Twentieth-century View', where we discard 'the precious but restricted direct and eye-witness evidence and move on to consider society overall'. This is supposed to show us the 'real', but just at this point things grow very obscure. What Goubert is mainly concentrating on in this section is the economic and financial system of the *ancien régime*: what types and groups were involved in it, what was the pattern of their careers, and what was the likely colour of their politics. These, the implication is, are the bourgeois according to the 'Twentieth-century View', and they do not correspond exactly to the bourgeois according to the eighteenth-century view: some people, for instance shopkeepers, are now left out,[9] and some have to be added, for instance the important group, 'the men with real power', who ultimately ran the system.

Now it is obviously awkward that the 'bourgeois' in the *ancien régime* should be a different set of people according to whether you are viewing them through eighteenth-century eyes or through twentieth-century ones; but at least the explanation (we assume) must be that in the one case what is in question is people's *status*, and in the other case their *politico-economic* role. But no, as we read on, we find that Goubert is still thinking about *status*; and what he feels he must do, apparently, is to construct his own twentieth-century status-system in rivalry with the *ancien régime* one. Now we say to ourselves, is not the creation of status-systems the prerogative of kings rather than of historians? And as it turns out, Goubert finds it cannot be done, and his chapter collapses in despairing rhetorical questions and in rebukes to those who believe it *can* be done. He describes the life-style of the great international merchant and comments (the italics are mine): 'The behaviour, sources of income and venturesome mentality of this type of wealthy bourgeois (*what else can we call him?*) locate him at the opposite pole to the "good bourgeois living on his income without working.".' But what about the so-called '*idéologues*' or critics of the government? Where do they stand in the '*social scale*'? Shall we term them, too, 'bourgeois', for want of a better name? No: 'to call them "bourgeois" throws no further light on this character'. Or, again, what about the 'enlightenment' intellectuals? Shall he label them 'bourgeois'? Or 'Does this gifted élite not transcend the usual subdivisions? Is it not the "political class" of the future, blurring the distinctions of birth and caste?' To this rhetorical question Goubert's answer—I suppose meaning 'yes'—is: 'The Revolution and its aftermath will show'—which makes us ask ourselves, what sort of a 'social scale' is this of the 1750s if it needs events of fifty years later to define people's position on it and another hundred and fifty years for the fact to be registered? They were dead by then, and it is no good the historian, in science-fiction fashion, pretending to launch himself back into the eighteenth century as Beau Brummel or social arbiter.

The truth seems obvious that you cannot hope to correct the social conceptions of a bygone age. Many historians, indeed, have accepted this. However, a way out has suggested itself to them. It is to employ a new concept, that of social 'strata' or 'stratification'. Standing aside, and disregarding for the moment the mutual social valuations of the people of a past society, the historian of today (so the theory runs) can discern the social 'stratification' of that society. The charm of the words 'strata' and 'stratification' is that they seem to suggest a structure which is visibly and indisputably *there*—so many social layers, superimposed like basalt and clay and coal—merely leaving it to the scholar to analyse what the layers are made of and how they came to be there and in that order. However, as you read on, you tend to find these scholars growing disloyal to their geological metaphor. It appears that, after all, it is not quite clear which the strata are, or where they lie. In fact it is a task requiring all a scholar's expertness to identify them; and, annoyingly, other scholars won't agree when he has done it. But gradually the doubt stirs in our mind: is our scholar behaving like a geologist at all? Is he identifying strata in a social rock-face, or is he not rather *classifying* or *grading*—classifying as you might, at will, classify the letters in your bureau 'Business', 'Personal', 'for Action', 'Pending', etc., or grading as you might grade eggs or undergraduate essays. In a word, is he not creating the strata himself, according to some principle, and then persuading himself that he has found them? He is ignoring the golden rule that, whereas it is for humans to classify* and grade, stratification is the prerogative of Nature.

The notion of 'strata' and 'stratification' does not really get us out of our difficulties, so we are brought back to that vexed word 'class'. A question has arisen among historians as to whether the terms 'class' and 'classes' can properly be used in regard to earlier periods—periods before ordinary people began to employ the terms. Now plainly, in my view, the debate rests on a fallacy. According to my theory, sorting people, including oneself, into 'classes' is a form of social *action* and hence not a proper part of a historian's activity at all—whether he be studying the tenth century or the nineteenth. Nevertheless the question has been taken seriously of late years, and some of the best thinking about 'class' has gone into it, so let us see how the debate has gone.

Those who say you should not apply the terms 'class' and 'classes' to the pre-nineteenth-century era tend to argue thus: the *thing* 'class' only came into existence in the nineteenth century, i.e. at the same moment that the *term* 'class' came into currency; hence to try to apply the term to earlier periods, like the seventeenth century or the Middle Ages, is an anachronism and bound to produce falsification. It is like taking the term 'caste' out of India and applying it to western Europe. J. H. Hexter is using this line of argument when he complains of R. H. Tawney's glib dealings with the 'the Tudor middle class'.

According to the exigencies of his [Tawney's] argument, the middle class is composed of men of the town and commerce, or of men of town and country alike; it includes small masters or it excludes them, includes the well-to-do copyholder or excludes him, includes the yeoman or excludes him, includes the gentry or excludes them. The conception of the middle class thus attains all the rigour of a rubber band.[10]

Those who take the opposite view (and they tend to be more or

---

* The rule remains true even in natural history. For instance an 'evolutionary' classification may be held to be more helpful to scientific enquiry than any other (though this is a point warmly disputed), but it will have no *logical* superiority. As Buffon stated memorably in the *Premier Discours* of his *Histoire naturelle*, how you construct your classification must depend entirely on what you want from it.

less Marxist in slant) argue that, for all the difficulty in applying 'class' concepts to earlier centuries or distant cultures, you just *have* to do it. 'Class' is a basic theoretic assumption, without which a historian can simply make no progress.

In his article, 'Eighteenth-century English society: class-struggle without class?', E. P. Thompson argues that 'class' is a 'historical category': that is to say, we have discovered the existence of 'class' and 'classes' and 'class-struggle' from studying the past and observing 'regularities of response to analogous situations'. One should not talk, as sociologists do, as if there were objective 'determinants' or criteria of class, whether of an economic kind, capable of measurement and quantification, or of a psychological kind (what class people *say* they belong to, as revealed in questionnaires etc.) Equally, it is a mistake to take a purely 'heuristic' approach, forming a model of capitalist productive relations and then 'deriving the classes that ought to correspond to this, and the consciousness that ought to correspond to the classes and their relative position'. All these approaches, says Thompson, are hopelessly prescriptive and 'static', and ignore the living and dynamic quality of 'class'—the 'classes' that emerge at different times and different places being always to some extent *sui generis* and unlike any other.

But what shall historians make of the fact, evidently important, that people only began to talk and think about 'class' ('class' became available to their 'cognitive system') in the early nineteenth century? At that moment, the concept of 'class' became a part of lived history, so would it not be wiser in historians to reserve the term for that period (and later)? Well no, says Thompson, this would be making life too easy for themselves. There are in fact two different senses in which a historian can employ the concept of 'class', and *both* are incumbent on him. There is an easy and 'empirical' one, in which he talks about 'class' because the people he is studying talk about it. And then there is a much harder one, not to be confused with the former, in which he uses it as a tool, an indispensable tool, for the analysis of all societies of whatever period.

That there are great logical and practical problems in using the concept of 'class' in this double way Thompson does not deny, indeed the only reason historians persevere with it, he says, is because no one has yet found an alternative. But in practice historians of ancient, medieval, and 'early modern' societies have used the term 'class', 'not without difficulty but with signal success'. There is, moreover, he says, a reason why this is so and why the practice is not so far-fetched as it seems. It is that the really important phenomenon is not 'classes' but 'class-struggle'. 'Classes' are the *result*, not the cause, of 'class-struggle'.

One respects E. P. Thompson, for he does honestly face problems; also one cheers for him for his swipes at what he calls 'the endless stupidities of quantitative measurement of classes'. However, there is a fallacy in his theory, which is (surely?) not difficult to spot. It is one thing to say that 'classes' are the result of 'class-struggle', not the cause of it—a perfectly reasonable remark—but quite another to picture a particular 'class-struggle' as taking a century, or five centuries, to produce a particular 'class' or 'classes'. Those are vast perspectives indeed! No social development, surely, takes quite that long? Or rather, this is not a profitable way to regard things; it too much recalls biblical exegetes, with their 'types' and millennial foreshadowings. But perhaps Thompson is saying that *some* class-struggles lead to the production of classes, but not all . . . ? No, it won't do: 'class-struggles' which are neither caused by classes nor result in classes—it is too moonshiny, too tortuous, too sophistical.

So what about the alternative theory?—that the *thing* 'class' only came into existence at the same time as the *word* did, i.e. in the early nineteenth century, and that accordingly a historian should use the word only when writing of this century and after. We may take Harold Perkin, in *The Origins of Modern English Society 1780–1880* (1969), as spokesman for this view. In a chapter called 'The Birth of Class' he writes that 'It was between 1815 and 1820 that the working class was born.' And (so he continues), the middle class was born at the same moment, though its birth was less 'traumatic'. The Corn Law of 1815 had served as proof that the aristocracy meant to govern merely in their own interest. The 'old society compact', by which the landed interest ruled on behalf of all the rest, was broken, and so the 'middle class' decided it must assert its own independent power.

What this moment in Britain witnessed, according to Perkin, was that most far-reaching consequence of the Industrial Revolution, 'the birth of a new class society'. A class society is 'characterized by class feeling, that is, by the existence of vertical antagonism between a small number of horizontal groups, each based on common source of income'. And its pattern contrasts diametrically with that of the 'Old Society', which was 'a hierarchical society in which men took their places in an accepted order of precedence, a pyramid stretching down from a tiny minority of the rich and powerful through ever larger and wider layers of lesser wealth and power to the great mass of the poor and powerless'. This 'hierarchy' was a finely graded one, of 'great subtlety and discrimination, in which men were acutely aware of their exact relation to those immediately above and below them, but only vaguely conscious except at the very top of their connections with those on their own level'.

The essence of class, as opposed to earlier social categorizations, says Perkin, is antagonism—'and not merely antagonism towards another class or classes but organized antagonism, with a nation-wide appeal to all members of one broad social level' (p. 209). Hence, politics in the new 'class' society were quite different from those of the Old Society. These latter had been 'interest politics'. In the Old Society you felt solidarity not with others at the same social level (for you were hardly conscious of them), but with the particular 'interest' (trade, industry, or profession) to which you belonged. These 'interests' are to be thought of as 'hierarchies within the general hierarchy of society'. They were parallel hierarchies and were often in competition, but under this system people did not fight for their own interests but allowed them to be fought for on their behalf, by those at the top.

One more point, to complete this crude summary of Perkin. Though classes are based on 'a common source of income', 'class' feeling (i.e. horizontal solidarity and vertical antagonism) 'transcends the common source of income'. This must be so (here Perkin is explicitly anti-Marxist) because the very same possessions and sources of income observable in nineteenth-century 'class' society 'may equally support, as in the old society . . . a totally different social structure'.

Perkin's scheme is certainly neat, so neat one is tempted to accept it. However, various difficulties arise. I will take the most important first. It would be foolish to deny that people in Victorian Britain talked a great deal about 'class', but this does not mean there was any agreement among them as to what they meant by the word. They were indeed, as we have seen with Mill, Thackeray, Cobden, Matthew Arnold, and the like, not much interested in sober definition, having something more urgent on their mind—viz., how to exploit the word for their own ends and for purposes of social action.

Thus part of what is wrong with Harold Perkin's historical scheme is that, on the matter of 'class', he is too glib; he seems too little to feel the problem in using those terms 'upper class', 'middle class', 'working class' and writes as if, in a quite unproblematic way, there simply *were* such things, looking much the same from whatever angle.

His method is to write history at the level of abstract entities. He depicts nineteenth-century British history as a sort of quadrille danced by the entities: 'the paternalist aristocratic ideal', 'the working-class ideal' (i.e. the ideal of the productive independent worker), 'the middle-class entrepreneurial ideal' and 'the middle-class professional ideal'. Now, I see no objection to writing history in terms of conflicting 'ideals'. What I question is the use of the epithets 'aristocratic', 'middle class', and 'working class'. As we see, they get Perkin into trouble at once. For it is exceedingly awkward for the 'middle class' to father two quite different, and indeed hostile, ideals—the acquisitive entrepreneurial one and the 'high-minded' professional one; and he has to resort to a complicated manœuvre to explain this, that of dubbing his altruists and philanthropists 'the forgotten middle class'. (Here, as so often, when 'class' terminology proves intractable, the user simply invents a new 'class'.) His scheme would be altogether less confusing (though it would also lose part of its charm and appear rather skeletal and *danse-macabreish*) if he dropped off those 'class' epithets; for the 'ideals' seem quite real and recognizable, much more real and sharply defined than the 'classes' from which they are supposed to emanate.

My other objection to Harold Perkin's scheme is that his account of the 'old society' sounds most implausible. Not that he is alone in it; and I don't mean that it is implausible in every respect. What fills me with scepticism is his notion of a 'hierarchical society'. How often do we hear of this 'hierarchical society' or 'social hierarchy', which is supposed to have existed at any time between AD 1000 and 1815, yet when one examines the concept it becomes quite hard to make sense of it. The subject is a large one, and it is one of those that I shall come on to in the second half of my book.

5

'Class' and the sociologists

The definition of 'class', a problem and a bone of contention for historians, becomes a scandal in sociology. Sociologists themselves lament the fact publicly and continually. They feel themselves more or less committed to the term 'class', yet, to a quite embarrassing degree, they cannot agree about how to define it. It is not just a matter of fine distinctions; they differ on a spectacular, and rather crippling, scale.

Ralf Dahrendorf speaks for many in the profession when he writes, in *Class and Class Conflict in Industrial Society*, that 'The history of the concept of class in sociology is surely one of the most extreme illustrations of the inability of sociologists to achieve even a minimum of consensus even in the modest business of terminological decisions.'[1] He quotes a small sample of conflicting definitions of 'the much abused concept of class', from T. H. Marshall, Richard Centers, R. M. MacIver, Fritz Croner and W. L. Warner and P. S. Lunt, remarking that 'Whoever reads these definitions may well be tempted to regard sociology as rather a frivolous discipline.' As for his remedy: it is 'back to Marx'. A stark choice faces the sociologist, argues Dahrendorf: 'either we renounce the discredited term "class" altogether and endeavour to find a less ambiguous set of terms, or we reject radically all definitions which depart from the original, i.e. Marxian, heuristic purpose and return to this source'.[2]

W. G. Runciman, in *Social Science and Political Theory*, writes in almost as severe a tone: 'academic sociologists have remained surprisingly inconsistent in their vocabulary . . . the literature is unnecessarily obscured by a welter of definitions and counter-definitions, discrepancies and tautologies which makes it impossible to tell precisely one theory from another, or even whether a given theory is a theory at all'.[3] The situation is almost nightmarish; and in fact, says Runciman, it is largely unnecessary. The remedy is 'back to Weber'. Max Weber, in his modification or expansion of Marx's theory of 'class', has really cleared up the matter of terminology—so that even if you differ from Weber in your social theories you can use his terminology to explain where you differ.

In a certain sense, the view to which Dahrendorf and Runciman

want to recall sociologists is the same one: it is that a 'class', whatever else it is, is not a community. We are not to think of a 'class' as a
collection of people familiarly linked by a common life-style and
social values, but rather as a *condition*—a shared situation of which
the members may or may not be conscious, and a base for possible
communal action. This, according to Dahrendorf and Runciman,
was the pure doctrine of Marx, who never diverged from it. (My
own impression, as will have been seen, is that he diverged from it
cheerfully when it happened to suit his purpose.) It is moreover, so
these writers hold, a *true* doctrine so far as it goes, only requiring
some augmentation. 'It is not so much that Weber wishes to mean
something different from Marx by "class",' says Runciman. 'It is
rather that he maintains that class, in the Marxian sense of economic class, is not the only dimension of social stratification . . . In
particular, we owe to Weber the crucial and still too often neglected
distinction between class and status.'[4] Or to quote Dahrendorf:

Wherever classes are defined by factors which permit the construction of a
hierarchical continuum, they are wrongly defined; i.e. the term has been
applied wrongly. Status, ranking by others, self-ranking, style of life, similar
economic conditions, and income level are all factors which define social
strata but not social classes. However one may interpret, extend, or improve
Marx, classes in his sense are clearly not layers in a hierarchical system of
strata differentiated by gradual distinctions.

The feeling both of Dahrendorf and of Runciman is that, unless they
can give the term 'class' a companion term or two—for Dahrendorf,
'social strata'; for Runciman, 'status-groups'—it is unusable. Dahrendorf, indeed, declares himself quite ready to give the term 'class' up
and only remains loyal to it as 'a tentative and reversible decision'.[5]

If we look at the series of essays, 'Theories of Class Structure',
which opens Bendix and Lipset's compendium *Class, Status and Power*
(1954), we shall see that Dahrendorf and Runciman did not exag-
gerate the disarray among sociologists. Joseph Schumpeter ('The
Problem of Classes') is sure that 'classes' *are* communities. A 'class'
is 'a special living social organism'; its members 'look out into the
same segment of the world, with the same eyes, from the same viewpoint, in the same direction'. Indeed, so palpable and flesh-and-
blood an entity is a 'class', its best definition is that it is (voluntarily)
endogamous: 'intermarriage prevails among its members, socially
rather than legally'.[6]

P. A. Sorokin ('What is a Social Class?') agrees with Schumpeter that 'classes' are real communities. As against Schumpeter, though, he does not allow that their members are defined totally by their 'class'. However, he is confident he can trace, not just vaguely but precisely, how different forms of collectivity dovetail. He can explain how a 'class' is constructed, which is by the 'coalescence' of three different types of 'bond'—an *occupational* bond, an *economic* bond, and the bond of 'belonging to the same basic stratum', with its 'essential rights and duties'; and he can explain similarly how membership of a 'class' relates to membership of a family, tribe, caste, order, or nation.[7]

For T. H. Marshall ('The Nature of Class Conflict'), a 'class' has as much or more to do with the differences between people as the likenesses: it is 'a force that unites into groups people who differ from one another, by overriding the difference between them'. 'Class' is a matter of *status*, a status awarded in virtue of certain *criteria*, such as property, income, education, and occupation. 'The institution of class teaches the members of a society to notice some differences and ignore others when arranging persons in order of social merit'.[8]

There is no doubt it is quite a battlefield. But if we stand back from the fray, we also notice something else. For whatever reason, the disagreements between these writers seem not just basic but elementary (and moreover it must be said the writers make what look rather like elementary logical errors). Let us take Schumpeter. He complains that the term 'class' has two quite distinct senses in the sciences, but that sociologists and economists 'annoyingly' often mix them up. A 'class' may mean any classification that a social scientist cares to make, or it can refer to a 'real' social phenomenon—i.e. 'special entities which we observe but which are not of our making'; and 'there is not the slightest connection between them as a matter of necessity'. Well, what puzzles one is that the warning should be necessary. Could any truth in the social sciences be more basic? The point is very simple. Say that you were a Treasury official and you decided to grade the national population, for tax purposes, by size of income: those earning up to £3,000, up to £4,000, up to £5,000 etc. The income groups that you would create in this manner would be 'real' in a certain sense, in that real people would be found in them; but it would seem very odd if you claimed to have *found* these groups, since you know very well that you have made them (and that you would have made different ones if you had graded up to £3,500, up to £5,500, up to £6,500 etc.) They are nothing to do with looking out of the window at the nation and noticing something about it.

The point is so clear that one would think Schumpeter's warning unnecessary. Nevertheless it is needed, as one finds only a few pages later in the same compendium, in Sorokin's 'What is a Social Class?' Sorokin's essay, from which I have quoted already, is a sort of hymn to the delights of definition. Is there, he asks, 'a specific multibonded group, different from the family, tribe, caste, order, or nation, that in modern times has exerted a powerful influence?' The answer is, 'yes, there is'; though whether we call this group a 'social class' or merely call it 'X' is, he says, a matter of indifference. He then proceeds to describe or define a 'class' according to an elaborate eight-point formula—congratulating himself on the 'superiority' of his definition to all previous efforts. Then a few sentences later he brings the whole edifice tumbling down in ruins. 'What kind of classes and how many', he asks, 'are found within the Western population throughout the history of the social class?' His answer is: it all 'depends upon how broad or narrow we make the occupational, the economic, and the stratification differences'.[9] Thus, after all, apparently, 'classes' are not something that we find, but something that we construct.

Let us look at Max Weber's essay ('Class, Status, Party'), which reveals another and more interesting *non sequitur*, or seeming *non sequitur*. As we have seen, in order to rescue the term 'class', which seems to be over-burdened, Weber decides to relieve it of some of its duties, transferring them to two companion terms: 'status-group' and 'party'. 'Status-groups' (unlike 'classes') are, according to Weber, 'normally communities' and are 'determined by a specific, positive or negative, social estimation of *honour*'. They are thus a quite different sort of thing from 'classes', which relate purely to 'market situation'—that is to say, to the kind of chance an individual possesses when bringing his property or services to the 'marketplace'. Further, 'status-groups' combine to form a larger entity, variously referred to by him as 'stratification by status', a 'status order', and a 'social order'.

His examples of 'status-groups' include a Swiss tax group, the members of which, it is reported, will dance only with one another; 'the street', i.e. residents of a certain street, who consider only the other inhabitants of the street as belonging to 'society' and as qualified for social intercourse; 'FFV', i.e. 'First Families of Virginia', or the actual or alleged descendants of the 'Indian Princess' Pocahontas, of the Pilgrim Fathers, or of the Knickerbockers; 'the members of almost inaccessible sects and all sorts of circles setting themselves apart by means of any other characteristics or badges'.[10]

It is an odd list, seeming not in fact to have much to do with honour. 'Inaccessible sects' appear to be quite out of place in it, for to form or to be asked to join such an exclusive sect seems precisely a way of turning your back on social 'honour'. (It was so explicitly on the part of the Quakers, with their doctrinaire refusal of hat-doffing and carnal dignities.) The same would seem to apply to Weber's 'all sorts of circles setting themselves apart'. As for 'the street': a more familiar term or concept might be 'set', as in 'the Cliveden set' or 'the Bloomsbury group'; and members of the Cliveden set and the Bloomsbury group certainly thought very well of themselves and were exclusive, having no wish to admit newcomers into their intimacy—but 'honour' hardly comes into the matter. Then those descendants of the Pilgrim Fathers or the Knickerbockers: they certainly laid claim to 'honour', in a whimsical way, and no doubt they amused themselves by forming clubs and performing rituals on Thanksgiving Day and other occasions; but did they, or did anyone, ever take their pretensions literally?

The point I am getting at is that, in any natural sense of the words, 'honour' and 'status' imply the existence of an honour-*system* and status-*system*; and there is no single system in which 'the street', the descendants of the Pilgrim Fathers or of the Knickerbockers, etc., can be assigned a place. However you arrange them together (but indeed, how would you begin to?) the result would not be a 'status order' or a 'stratification by status' or 'social order'. Moreover, just the same is true of Dahrendorf's 'hierarchical system of strata differentiated by gradual distinctions'. 'Hierarchical', 'strata', 'gradual': these phrases conjure up some single order of valuation, whereas what one finds in any concrete human situation is a variety of conflicting or unrelated value-systems.

Now, as we saw, these phrases were resorted to by Weber and others as a way of rescuing the term 'class'—a term breaking down under its burdens and requiring assistance from other terms if it is to carry on. The trouble is, the new terms add to the confusion; and the root of the trouble, I suggest, is still that formidable word 'class', which plays such tricks with its users, when they are not themselves using it to play tricks with. Sociologists, in this like historians, have not taken its measure, or perceived how inveigling and masterful a term it is; thus their efforts to escape its toils merely entangle them further.

Peter Calvert, in *The Concept of Class*, suggests a beautifully simple explanation of the difficulties, the 'scandal', besetting sociologists. It is that 'social class' belongs in a category defined by the philosopher

W. B. Gallie as 'essentially contested concepts': that is to say, 'concepts the proper use of which inevitably involves endless disputes about their proper use on the part of their users'.[11] Gallie gives a number of defining characteristics for such a concept: it must be *appraisive* 'in the sense that it signifies or accredits some kind of valued achievement'; this achievement must be internally complex; it must, *initially*, be describable in various different ways; it must be of a kind to admit of modification in the lights of changing circumstances; it must derive from an original exemplar, whose authority is acknowledged by all users; and it must be plausible to claim that continuous competition about how to use the concept is the best way of furthering the 'achievement'. As possible examples of essentially contested concepts, he cites Art, Democracy, Social Justice, and 'adherence to or participation in a particular religion' (e.g. the concept of 'a Christian life').

Now if Gallie is right, and there are such things as essentially contested concepts, could 'class' be one of them? It is an attractive idea, and 'class' seems to satisfy most of Gallie's conditions. The chief problem is whether, in any reasonable sense, 'class' can be called an 'achievement'. Peter Calvert persuades himself that it can but does not quite convince me. Gallie's use of the word 'achievement' is certainly very broad, but it entails some general agreement that Art, Democracy, Social Justice, a Christian life, etc. are a *good thing* and this is not precisely what anyone would say about 'class' (though they might secretly think it, for 'unholy' reasons). Indeed, as I have tried to show, 'class' stands in a very strange relationship to the appraisal or evaluation question. By its 'scientific'-sounding overtones (its gesture towards natural-history classification) it seems to be claiming to be value-free; whilst from another angle, at least in its English version, it is purely and simply a matter of social value-judgement, asserting nothing about the members of a 'class' other than that they are higher or in the middle or lower. Again, in its Marxist version, 'class' is not an 'achievement' but an evil fact, to be got rid of—though a subtext says that, to achieve a classless society what is first needed is for class identities to be sharpened and class-conflict exacerbated.

Certainly, if 'class' were an essentially contested concept, it would explain much. It would help remove the 'worry' I have spoken of; and Dahrendorf and Runciman would have to withdraw their complaints against their colleagues, or at least frame them differently. I imagine they would not too much welcome the idea, though, or be very eager to accept Calvert's view, that 'it is a waste of time to attempt to establish a meaning for it ['class'] that will command universal acceptance, for the value of the term lies in the fact that that task is impossible'. The trouble is, it is hard to see what use a sociologist could make of an 'essentially contested concept'. It doesn't seem the sort of tool he is accustomed to handling, and it might make him feel he must give up 'class' altogether.

Let us assume then, that he does not adopt this escape-route. How, then, is he to explain to himself the 'scandal'—I mean, he and his colleagues' failure to agree on how to use quite basic terms? I will offer a mild suggestion. It is, that calling things by the names 'class', 'status', 'stratum', etc. is *not* the same as calling them 'X', 'Y', and 'Z'. Language, after all, has its laws, and it is not true that any word can be used to mean anything. Thus, words like 'class' and 'status' carry certain implications that are inescapable. A 'class' necessarily implies the existence of a classifier, and this leads to the question, who is this classifier? Who is doing the classing? Similarly, the word 'status' necessarily raises the question, 'Status in whose eyes?'. (As we saw with Weber and his 'status-groups', it makes no sense to speak of individuals or groups as bestowing honour or status on themselves.) We have the spectacle of a lot of people classifying one another, and a lot of people bestowing honour upon one another, and it is for the sociologist—somewhat like the Henry Jamesian novelist concerned with 'viewpoint'—to sort out the logic or 'grammar' of these operations. It is to answer such questions as 'Who is doing the classifying?', 'Who is doing the bestowing of honour?' that sociologists exist. On the other hand, in a certain bad sort of sociological writing, language is used not to answer these questions, but precisely to cover them up and make it seem as if they had already been answered. There is a sort of shimmer of half-meaning in such writing, where words like 'class', 'status', 'stratum', 'hierarchy' are just sufficiently set adrift from secure definition to preclude the awkward questions 'Who?' and 'How?' or 'By what mechanism?'.

I am thinking, for instance, of that essay by Sorokin, 'What is a Social Class?' (see pp. 64–6). Consider, just as one example among many, how he uses the word 'bond':

The specific characteristic of the social class is the coalescence of occupational and economic bonds plus the bond of belonging to the same basic stratum, whose properties are defined by the totality of its essential rights and duties, or by its privileges and disfranchisements, as compared with those of other classes.[12]

'Economic bonds', as he goes on to explain, means 'similarity of economic position'; and 'similar economic position' seems to mean here not much more than similar income. So why 'bonds'? As a moment's reflection will tell us, to have the same income as other people does not, by itself, constitute any sort of bond. For all we know, Iris Murdoch may enjoy the same income as the Lord Mayor of Bristol, but this does not create a bond between them.

That word 'coalescence', though! How it epitomizes the duty, and also the dream, of sociologists: I mean, to explain how the innumerable different relationships in which an individual stands (legal relationships, family relationships, relationships in a chain of command etc.) are to be seen as dovetailing—as 'coalescing', if that is the word. One favourite assumption is that they somehow all add up to compose a single 'order' in which the individual has a single 'position' or 'place'. It seems to me quite a false assumption, indeed logically impossible, but there is no doubt it has had a large following and is enshrined in such phrases as 'the social order', 'the social hierarchy'. It was such a notion, as propounded by Harold Perkin, that I was questioning at the end of the last chapter. That it should have had a following in the past is not difficult to understand. It was, after all, a theme continually harped upon by preachers and enjoined, often with menaces, by the powers-that-be—so that a citizen of the late Middle Ages or the Tudor and Stuart period had plenty of motive for believing it, or at least paying lip-service to it. What seems more curious is that modern historians and sociologists should subscribe to it.

Nevertheless they do, as I have already noted once or twice; and I will end this chapter with another and rather striking example. It is from Roland Mousnier's *Les Hiérarchies sociales de 1450 à nos jours* (Social Hierarchies from 1450 to the Present Day).[13] It will show how the notion of a single 'order', offering a single 'place' or 'position' to each individual, goes along with a certain rubbing-off-of-the-corners of and dissolving of all sharpness of meaning in the terms 'hierarchy', 'stratum', and 'status'.

Social value-judgements, writes Mousnier, 'are based on a variety of criteria', some of which are more vague than others.

These criteria fall into categories, giving different ladders or scales of social stratification, which are bound [*liées*] together and normally are combined in the attribution of rank. They often exhibit asymmetries [*écarts*]: the same person may find himself highly placed on one ladder and low on another.

We need, says Mousnier, to distinguish four sorts of ladder of social stratification, viz., *legal stratification*, *social status*, *economic hierarchy* and *power*—no, five, because, so he remembers, there is also *ideological stratification*. He proceeds to define these five ladders, and then continues, to our surprise:

We have to draw up [*dresser*] these different ladders or scales and examine the relationships between them, their correlations and their deviations, if we are to discern the social stratification of a given society and situate an individual or a particular group within it.

So after all, apparently a given society *has* an overall 'social stratification', and an individual or a particular group can be 'situated' within it. The warning that 'the same person may find himself highly placed on one ladder and low on another' did not mean what we took it to mean, and it is to be revealed that, in some higher vision, the many will become one. Indeed the argument turns into a rebuke to his fellow-thinkers for not doing as he has done, or paying proper attention to all those five 'scales':

This is what many politicians and sociologists have neglected to do when trying to define the notion of social class. They have done so sometimes on political, sometimes on professional, grounds, forgetting that a social stratification is the result of the combination of these three factors and of some others . . .

All these theories seem to derive from an inadequate analysis of social realities, from a partial view of these realities. A more thorough social analysis shows that, to know a social stratum, it is necessary to combine several *ensembles* of factors bound together [*liés*] by an interplay [*jeu*] of reciprocal actions and reactions, of which the chief ones are social status, economic situation, and power.[13]

Well, all one can say is, by putting it this way Mousnier makes us want to give up on the spot, it all seems so very difficult. For how on earth are we going to combine, or add up, or equate those five different ladder-positions? In what kind of higher-order system can they turn out to constitute a single 'position' after all? It is just here that we need help; and one thing is plain, we shall receive none from Mousnier himself, apart from the injunction to go away and do it. This suggests to me that he has never tried it himself, and that it is not possible, and (what is more) that it is not to the point.

PART 2

BEFORE 'CLASS', AND AFTER?

'And oranges, cactuses, crystals and mud? and the bacteria inside Mr Sorley? No, no, this is going too far. We must exclude someone from our gathering, or we shall be left with nothing.'

(E. M. Forster, *A Passage to India*)

6

✳

The 'social hierarchy'

Harold Perkin's account of 'the old society' was that it was a 'hierarchical society in which men took their places in an accepted order of procedures, a pyramid stretching down from a tiny minority of the rich and powerful through ever larger and wider layers of lesser wealth and power to the great mass of the poor and powerless'. In the old world, according to him, there was a finely graded 'hierarchy, of great subtlety and discrimination, in which men were acutely aware of their exact relation to those immediately above and below them'. Give or take a detail or two, this picture of pre-industrial England seems to be fairly standard and to be endorsed by modern historians as well as old-fashioned ones, by Marxist historians as well as anti-Marxist ones. (And, of course, it is not only England of which it is said. We find de Tocqueville writing: 'Each citizen of an aristocratic society has his fixed station, one above another.')[1]

The theory looms large in the writings of Peter Laslett and Lawrence Stone. In *The World We Have Lost* (1965) Laslett tried to discredit the idea of 'class-conflict' in Tudor and Stuart England. 'Classes', he argues, is not a term that fits that earlier England; what characterized it, rather—and what for good or evil we have now quite lost—was a 'coherent status-system'.

Historians used to write in much the same vein of the feudal period. 'The king, the peer, the knight, the yeoman, the villein, the merchant, the labourer, the artisan, the various sorts of person in orders, all occupied definite and legally fixed places in the hierarchy of society.' So wrote Holdsworth in his *History of English Law*, and very similar words are used by many historians writing today. Others are more cautious and say that this was, at least, how things appeared to men and women in the past. Perez Zagorin writes in *The Court and the Country* that:

To the observation of the sixteenth and seventeenth centuries, society appeared as a hierarchy or orders or degrees of men, graduated from the prince at the top, through the peerage, gentry and other estates, down to the artificers, husbandmen, and labourers at the bottom. Such was the conception everywhere implicit in the religious, didactic and imaginative literature of the age, and incorporated as well as in formal accounts of the society by contemporary thinkers.[2]

Now, I think one needs to distrust this idea, in all its various forms, and partly because it suggests a wrong notion as to what was new about 'class'.

The underlying idea of the 'social hierarchy' or 'hierarchy of society' seems to be that there was some single ladder of social position, recognized and accepted by all. However, the trouble is, if you were to take this literally and try actually to draw the ladder out on paper, you would get at once into the most serious difficulties. Let us think of Holdsworth's feudal society. We receive a picture of much up-and-downness—the king seems sky-high as compared with the labourer—but otherwise the relationships of the various categories seem quite a tangle. Say that the 'villein' or the merchant holds some land, then his lord of the manor may be a knight, but on the other hand—if the land is monastic—he may be an abbot. Does not even this already upset the idea that 'villeins' or merchants, in general, had a fixed 'position in the social hierarchy', i.e. a fixed position in regard to knights and abbots in general? Then, if the villein, or the merchant, has a landholding relationship to an abbot, he will also as a layman have a spiritual relationship to his parish priest. Are we to believe that these two relationships, and the various other relationships he stands in, add together in some mysterious way to define a single 'social position'? Or consider, how could you hope to find a single 'hierarchy' or ladder on which Chaucer's Knight, Squire, Yeoman, Monk, Merchant, Clerk, Sergeant, Haberdasher, Carpenter, Webber, Dyer, Tapycer, Cook, Shipman, Doctor of Physic, Wife of Bath, Parson of a Town, Plowman, Reve, Miller, Summoner, Pardoner, Manciple, Miller, Reeve, and Host all have an allotted and agreed place? A Shipman would probably never have given a thought to his position relative to a Monk or a Merchant, and why should he? But even if he had, his relative position to these would depend upon the context; it would be different, no doubt, on his ship from what it was inside a monastery or a guildhall. This is not to say there were no systems of status in the fourteenth century, but that, precisely, they existed in the plural, and the idea of them resolving themselves into a single scale appears a delusion.

Of course if a shipman, a monk and a merchant were brought together on some formal occasion, like a banquet or a funeral procession, it would be necessary for somebody to work out a system of precedence, a system for that particular occasion. (Chaucer himself has given the Knight the place of honour in the *Canterbury Tales*, both in order of appearance and stylistically.) This is a perfectly familiar problem; and the master of ceremonies at a banquet or funeral would work out a seating or walking order as best he could, with the aid of Tables of Precedence and handbooks of etiquette. And the essential point about 'Precedence', at least as applied in such cases, is that it cannot be continuously systematic; it must contain patches of system, interrupted by fissures, which have to be bridged by arbitrary rulings and rule-of-thumb. This indeed is exactly what it is about; it is the casuistry of social ordering and a method of adjusting conflicting systems.

This misleading notion of a 'social hierarchy' is, I think, partly the fruit of an abuse of the word 'hierarchy'. It seems a mistake, or anyway a pity, to use the term 'hierarchy'—as is often done—to include everything in the nature of a ladder or up-and-down gradation. For thereby one loses a most useful sense (the root one) of 'hierarchy'—namely as a chain of authority, potential or actual. The term, meaning 'priestly rule', first came into use to denote the successive grades of bishop, priest and deacon—i.e. of a chain of subordination in regard to authority, here spiritual—and some memory of this meaning seems intrinsic to it. It is in this familiar sense that we apply the word 'hierarchy' to the army (general, colonel, lieutenant-colonel etc.), to business organization, and to the civil service.

Other features too seem to be naturally included in the meaning of 'hierarchy'. A hierarchy (unlike a stratification) is *homogeneous*. (The angelic hierarchy is composed entirely of angels, and the military hierarchy is composed entirely of officers—apart from one group, known as 'other ranks', whose sole and complete definition is that they are not officers, or at least not commissioned officers.) A human hierarchy is *composed of posts or offices*. A hierarchy (unlike a stratification) is *made, not found*. (God, it is to be presumed, created the angelic hierarchy, he did not just find it there. And there would be no logical absurdity in speaking of a hierarchy to which no one had ever yet actually belonged.) And finally, since it is made not found, a hierarchy is *complete*. (What would be the point of creating an incomplete hierarchy?)

Thus the phrase 'the social hierarchy' conveys the slightly comic and anachronistic picture of a nation run like a regiment or a business organization. Whereas in fact any nation, whether in the fourteenth century or the twentieth, must comprise a large number of different hierarchies, and members of the nation may occupy posts

in several of them simultaneously—perhaps ranking high in one and
low in another. Nor is it clear that medieval or Tudor and Stuart
society were any more keen on hierarchies than twentieth-century
society, where (in industry and administration) they are regarded as
essential. (Michel Foucault, in *Surveiller et Punir*, has shown that
'hierarchical surveillance' grew greatly in importance in the eighteenth century.) Maybe what has helped foster the idea of the 'hierarchical society' is the fact that, in the first feudal age, the
seigneurial 'household'—households tend to be organized roughly
hierarchically—was the most conspicuous model of social organization. It would foster the thought 'How nice if the nation could run
itself like a household'—a kind of *per impossibile* sentiment fostered by
the warring of rival households.

Let us go back to Harold Perkin's phrase 'the accepted order of
precedence'. It reads rather oddly, for when one is actually reading
about the seventeenth and eighteenth centuries, and for that matter
the fifteenth century, what strikes one is the enormous energy
expended on *contesting* 'the accepted order of precedence'; how
people would jostle one another in processions or churches or ban-
queting-halls, or wherever they happened to come together in public, and how prone they were to take one another to law over matters
of precedence in civil or ecclesiastical courts.

Of course it may be answered that this merely goes to show how
real and vivid the 'social hierarchy' was to people in the past. But
this would be another confusion engendered by the too-vague use of
the word 'hierarchy'. Taking the word in my sense, at least, what
emerges is that 'hierarchy' and 'precedence' are not allied but contrasted concepts. (We should remember that precedence is not concerned with 'position', but with an occurrence, viz., that someone
should precede another through a doorway or in a procession.) Thus
people are worried about precedence precisely when, or in so far as,
they are not part of a hierarchy. A colonel need have no worries
about precedence vis-à-vis a lieutenant-colonel, nor a bishop vis-à-
vis a priest—not, at least, in the circumstances of their professional
life. Where precedence-disputes arise is in all those other (and
innumerable) situations where two or more value-systems cross. As
between two ex-lord mayors, should precedence in certain contexts
follow seniority in age or seniority of appointment as Lord Mayor?
Does his office as Chief-President of the Parlement, at the court of
Louis XIV, give M. Novion the right to seat himself in front of one
of the princes of the blood?[3] Such is the pattern of precedence-

disputes; and essentially they have no meaning outside of a given and very narrow social context. Who, not living in or near a chartered borough, is going to worry his head over competing claims to precedence between ex-lord mayors?*

It may be seen, though, how attractive a thought it would be to contestants in precedence-disputes if appeal could be made to a *universal* and God-given social ordering. Here we see the origin of the notion of a 'social hierarchy'. Quite impossible logically, it is nevertheless very potent rhetorically—as law-givers and preachers have not been slow to discover, so that many a statute or royal edict will prescribe due respect to 'degree' and social 'station'. The law and judiciary, indeed, have handled the matter in a characteristically pragmatic way. For example: the Earl Marshal's court, which rose to prominence in the 1630s, was happy to hear actions in which one man sued another for denying that he was a 'gentleman'; but it would decide the issue of gentility on the most perfectly non-committal of grounds, viz., whether or not, for a space of years, the plaintiff's neighbours had *called* him, or his father, a 'gentleman'. As G. D. Squibb puts it in *The High Court of Chivalry* (1959), 'The definition of a gentleman in the Court of Chivalry seems to have been "one who is reputed to be a gentleman"—a definition reminiscent of the well-known definition of an archdeacon as one who performs archidiaconal functions.' By this strategy, the court was able to attach moral weight to the 'social hierarchy' idea, and thereby execute the wishes of the Caroline 'establishment', without embarking on the awkward task of *explaining* it.

A point to get hold of is that to 'believe in' or to 'accept' some idea are phrases susceptible of more than one interpretation. One may believe in, or accept, the idea of perpetual motion, but this does not mean that one can explain how it works. The same is true of the 'social hierarchy'. It is undoubtedly true that commentators, from medieval times onwards, asserted the existence of a 'social

---

* It is my impression that failure to perceive the distinction and opposition between hierarchy and precedence causes confusion in discussions of *caste* in India, including even Louis Dumont's in *Homo Hierarchicus*. Dumont, though he corrects H. H. Risley, an organizer of the 1901 Census in India, for believing that 'hierarchy consisted in a linear order' ('he [Risley] did not see that this order was only the consequence, not to say the by-product, of a hierarchical opposition'), does not seem ready to admit how very wild the notion of such a 'linear order' really is. On Dumont's own evidence, even to begin to picture an 'order' among Hindu castes one would need a three-dimensional model of the complexity of Watson and Crick's 'double helix'. That for a given purpose, like a village wedding-feast (or indeed a National Census), somebody (an anxious host or a census-official) will have to cut the knot and work out an order of precedence, seems an entirely different matter.

hierarchy' (though not in those words) and frequently complained, if they were preachers, or if they were men feeling their own position threatened, that people were not observing their 'place'. But when we say that they 'believed' in this hierarchy, what we really mean is that they believed that some such thing *ought* to exist, over and above the tangle of social relationships in which they were actually enmeshed. They were, for whatever reason, making a rhetorical assertion, and it is not for us to take them literally—for the good reason that you would not be able to do so if you tried. It is this, and not any accusation that such beliefs represented 'false conscious-ness', that should make us sceptical of an assertion such as Perez Zagorin's:

Nor should we imagine that the notion of status was merely a myth, an illu-sory form of consciousness, falsifying for those who thought in its categories the reality in which they lived. However it might distort by idealizing a sys-tem of inequality, it nevertheless corresponded to an objectively-given struc-ture of distinctions.[4]

That 'objectively-given structure of distinctions' turns out to be decidedly vague, indeed altogether foggy anywhere but at the top and the bottom. The same is true of it as was said by Sylvia Thrupp of the medieval theory of 'ranks':

the theory had not been concerned to define status relationships in any detail. The philosophical thought that lay behind it was content with an ideal picture. The set hierarchy that it demanded was not actualised except in the higher ranks of the nobility. The theory was most easily expounded by presenting dramatically contrasted types, such as the lord or the knight, on the one hand, as against the manual labourer. In consequence the relative status of groups intermediate between these was left altogether ambiguous.[5]

One may perceive here the attraction of the scheme known as the 'Great Chain of Being', according to which the universe exhibits a continuous chain or ladder of creatures, extending without break from the worm to the angel, with Man occupying exactly the mid-way position. This scheme takes us into the region of the purely hypothetical, and in such a region there is of course nothing to stop us from positing a chain or 'hierarchy', in which A is linked to B and B to C in a neat and single ascending order—as opposed to the tangled criss-cross found in real life, by which A is directly linked to B for certain purposes and directly linked to C for others. With such a scheme as the Great Chain there is no need for rules of precedence, to adjust different systems of value to one another. And the only trouble with it, as Dr Johnson pointed out, is that it is not a chain, since it would hold just as well (or just as badly) if half the links dropped out. 'No system can be more hypothetical than this', said Johnson, 'and perhaps no hypothesis more absurd.'[6]

I will give one further illustration of my point, from Richard Gough's *History of Myddle*.[7] In 1700 the Shropshire farmer Richard Gough had the idea of writing the history of his parish by tracing the history of each family within it, dealing with them in the order of their pews or kneelings in the parish church. The historian David Hey, in a book about Myddle, *An English Rural Community* (1974), takes Gough's account as proving that 'the social gradations within the community were formalized by the strictness of the seating arrangements' and that 'the exhibition of these social gradations on Sundays and festivals was the unifying factor in the life of the community'. It is this, says Hey, 'as much as anything else, that marks off Tudor and Stuart Myddle from modern society'. (I detect an echo here of *The World We Have Lost*.) When we look at Gough's own account, though, and at his diagram of pews and their owners, we get a surprise. For Gough himself lays claim to kneelings in four separate pews, dotted all over the church, and something similar is true for several other families. Thus, if the seating arrangements exemplify the social order in Myddle, this social order seems to be rather a strange one.

That the kneelings should be so distributed is, in fact, not too difficult to explain. It was partly the result of the system in operation in Shropshire and many other parts of England, by which pews went with houses; so that if a house changed hands, the right to sit in a given pew changed hands also. It also reflected the fact that in 1658 certain influential parishioners had formed themselves into a vestry and sorted out the seating arrangements to suit themselves. It was indeed a fact with a complicated history, illustrating exactly that complicated tangle of superimposed and conflicting relationships which is found in all concrete social situations. It does, however, make Gough's diagram look extremely unlike a ladder, and more like a rather intricate piece of knitting.

But anyway, Gough himself explicitly disclaims any attempt to set out his fellow-parishioners in an ideal order of social precedence. 'I hope noe man will blame mee for not nameing every person according to that which hee conceives is his right and superiority in the seats in Church, because it is a thing impossible for any man to know.'[8] Priority in a pew, he explains, does not necessarily correspond to social priority outside the pew[9] and if anyone wants to try and establish the ideal social order in Myddle, he says, it might help him to consider how much each parishioner pays in church-rates. Then, having done so, he could examine their pedigrees. And all this might lead to some 'probable conjecture'.[10] Thus Gough invokes at least three separate criteria of social ordering, liable to disagree with one another. And all that the scene in the church-nave actually exhibited unambiguously each Sunday was that grander people tended to be seated near to the pulpit and humbler people in the opposite extremity of the nave.

There is a lesson for us in this, and it is the same one that was expressed by Sylvia Thrupp, viz., that the famous 'social hierarchy' of pre-industrial times was quite vague and fuzzy everywhere save at its top and bottom and indeed belonged mainly to rhetoric. Thus it is somewhat of a comedy, or so it seems to me, when Peter Laslett and Lawrence Stone take it literally, and labour to draw out the seventeenth-century 'status-system' for us on paper, with the help of the well-known table of Gregory King, devised in the 1690s. Lawrence Stone, in an article 'Social Mobility in England, 1500 to 1700',[11] describes the 'status-hierarchy' of sixteenth-century England as a clear-cut affair, quite unlike the 'loose competitive status-agglomeration to which we are accustomed today'. Though (tiresomely for lovers of neatness) there existed, so he says, 'a few completely non-integrated groups—artists and stage-players for example', and 'four semi-independent occupational hierarchies' (the merchants, the lawyers, the clergy and the administrators). Nevertheless, he asserts, 'the vast mass of the population was fitted into a single hierarchy of status defined by titular rank, and to a certain extent by legal and fiscal privilege'. Well, it strikes us at once that for a 'status-hierarchy' so comprehensive as he paints it, those vexing non-joiners the merchants, lawyers, clergy, and administrators seem a pretty large exception! Then it turns out, there is a troublesome dearth of status-names, (as distinct from mere occupational descriptions). When one comes down to it, there are no more than three, viz., 'nobleman', 'gentleman' and 'yeoman', with 'esquire' as a distinctly shadowy and elusive fourth. So to give the 'hierarchy' even a modicum of amplitude he has to pad it out with all the ranks of the peerage (duke, earl, viscount, etc.), though one would not normally think of these as separate *statuses*. ('Nobleman' is a status; 'earl' is a rank.) And after all this, his table does not prove what it is supposed to; indeed it proves the opposite, i.e. that 'the vast mass of the population' was *not* fitted into a single hierarchy of status defined by titular rank. Likewise Peter Laslett, in a 'Chart of rank and status— Stuart England',[12] only manages to produce anything resembling a ladder by drawing on at least four different systems of classification: rank ('earl' etc.), status ('nobleman' etc.), occupation ('husband-man' etc.) and economic description ('pauper' etc.). One begins to be reminded of that Chinese encyclopaedia in the Borges story, which classifies animals as: '(a) belonging to the Emperor (b) embalmed (c) tame (d) sucking pigs . . . (h) included in the present classification'.[13]

To return once again to Harold Perkin: if, as the evidence shows, people in pre-industrial society spent so much of their time in quarrelling with their neighbours about honour and precedence, where is the great contrast posited by Perkin between their way of life and the 'antagonism' of modern 'class' society? It lay, it will be answered, in the fact that in 'class' society the antagonism is *organized*, i.e. is political. Or we may rewrite this answer as saying: quarrels about precedence and honour are silly nonsense, not a serious matter like political conflict. Now, this is a tenable view. But, seeing how much passion people in the past put into such quarrels, it was plainly not their view.

At this point a tempting thought presents itself: perhaps quarrels about precedence and honour are, precisely, an expression of impotence and are the outlet for people deprived of political influence? But that theory will not work either: for, though the great men at Charles I's court were probably not much more precedence-and-honour mad than anyone else in the country, they were certainly not less so. We are thus forced to conclude that political conflict, and conflict over honour and precedence, are separate phenomena, not *necessarily* connected, though of course often connected in practice. There is a form of human conflict and competition which we can call 'purely social'. Perhaps no one ever doubted this, for it is such a large and obvious fact, but it is worth being clear about it, since it is part of the influence of Marx to make us look for the political everywhere. The point is going to be important to us when we come back to 'class' in the last part of this book; for the immediate origins of 'class' (that is to say, of the concept of 'class') were political, and the 'purely social' elements that it gathered into itself were much more ancient in origin.

*

7

Honour and the *honnête*

We are not coming at the concept of 'class' rightly, then, if we picture the breakdown of a settled and understood social order and its replacement by a new, strivingly competitive arrangement known as 'class'. For under scrutiny that settled social system with its 'finely graded distinctions', dislimns and grows shadowy, resolving into a rhetoric. It was not a system but rather an assertion that such a system existed (for all that its details might be rather hard to find out), or anyway that there *ought* to be such a system. Thus from one point of view ancient 'social hierarchy' and modern 'class' are much of a muchness, both being essentially rhetorical in nature. From another point of view, however, they differ fundamentally, in that the 'social hierarchy' was officially sanctioned, and weightily prescribed in many a statute and episcopal injunction; whereas 'classes' are considered a democratic 'people''s own invention, and governments—far from aspiring to give them legal force—are very cautious about even acknowledging their existence. (The Registrar-General's *Classification of Occupations* (1970) makes use of the term 'class', but, for reasons we have no trouble at all in understanding, does not even admit the existence of an 'upper class'.[1] One can imagine the scandal, and questions asked in Parliament, if it had done so.)

It is this matter of sanction that seems most necessary for us to take hold of. Of course words like 'rank' and 'orders' lingered on, upon some statesmen's lips, well into the middle of the nineteenth century, but the will to impose them had gone. If citizens wanted to imagine themselves, or imagine others, in the form of 'classes', it was their democratic right to do so: the monopoly in social rhetoric had been abolished, or at least had changed hands. In the vast and sudden transformation which overtook Britain round about the beginning of the nineteenth century, this was a factor of considerable importance.

That the chosen new rhetoric or concept should be 'class' is very important and indeed partly what this book is about. To help in understanding it, one needs to ponder the relationship of the concept 'class' to the older concepts of 'rank', 'order', 'degree', 'station', etc.

It is usual with sociologists to contrast 'class' with 'status', a term which seems to fit those older concepts, and to speak of an earlier 'status-system' as being supplanted in the nineteenth century by a 'class-system'. However, as I have argued (pp. 66–7), 'status' has proved a very equivocal and contentious term. Thus we shall get on better perhaps by thinking about 'honour'. Let me try out a broad hypothesis: that we are to picture social relations as moving from a system of 'honour'—in which some boon, some positive, some absolute is being apportioned—to a system of 'class', which is concerned entirely with the relative, is indeed a system purely of exclusion.

Honour as 'What is due'

Honour, we may say, is concerned with what is 'due' to individuals, and in theory it would be possible for everyone to receive his or her due, without prejudice to the claims of others. There is always, by definition, enough honour to go round. (I am here talking of honour from the point of view of the giving or receiving of it, not of its 'shame' side, the defending or losing of it.) Let me quote the duc de Saint-Simon's obituary tribute to *Monsieur*, the brother of Louis XIV:

The bulk of the Court regretted *Monsieur*, for it was he who set all pleasure a-going; and when he left it, life and merriment seemed to have disappeared likewise. Setting aside his obstinacy with regard to the Princes, he loved the order of rank, preferences, and distinctions: he caused them to be observed as much as possible, and himself set the example. He loved great people; and was so affable and polite, that crowds came to him. The difference which he knew how to make, and which he never failed to make, between everyone according to his position, contributed greatly to his popularity. In his receptions, by his greater or less, or more neglectful attention, and by his words, he always marked in a flattering manner the differences made by birth and dignity, by age and merit, and by profession.[2]

'Precedence' as described here is a system of positive (and in a sense universal) pleasure—or it would be so, if only other people would not so crassly trespass on one's due rights: but, for all the claim that courtiers might nurse on behalf of their family or their 'order', and for all the grudge that some like Saint-Simon might harbour against the absolutist regime, they accepted the rays of royal favour, i.e. a certain given proportion of those rays, as the full settlement of their 'due'. As Saint-Simon describes it, *Monsieur*'s scrupulous attention to 'rank, preferences, and distinctions' was designed, above all, to provide enjoyment—and in theory enjoyment for *everyone*. It was in the same spirit that, at the coronation of Richard II, the claims of the Mayor of London to serve the king with a goblet of wine before he dined, and of a selected group of citizens to help the chief butler at the dinner itself, were granted by the king 'to make their hartis merier' (and in token of financial favours to come).[3] Thus, too, the Chandos herald writes admiringly of the Black Prince's court at Bordeaux: 'there abode all nobleness, all joy and jollity, largesse, gentleness and honour.'[4] One remembers, too, Proust's Françoise and her sheer aesthetic delight in aristocratic technicalities:

Françoise—to whom one could talk about wireless or the genius of Napoleon without managing to hold her attention or even for a moment interrupt her emptying of the grate or laying of the table—on hearing such [aristocratic] particulars and learning that the younger son of the duc de Guermantes was usually called Prince of Orléans would exclaim, enraptured, 'How lovely!', as if at the sight of a stained-glass window.[5]

J. G. Peristiany, discussing the ethical theories of 'honour and shame' societies, writes: 'It is interesting to note that it is not the struggle for honour but the struggle for material possessions which breeds envy and temptations which endanger man's soul.'[6]

As I hardly need say, codes of honour and concern for 'face' are far from being an exclusively aristocratic perquisite. Peasant societies, as is well known, tend to be ruled by codes of Honour and Shame; and in England (of course, a notoriously litigious country), people of humble circumstances have from early times been fond of suing for slander and defamation. According to J. A. Sharpe[7] there was a positive 'explosion' of such litigation in the period 1560–1730, much of it instituted by 'the middling sort of rural people'. He records an incident in Yorkshire in 1696, when 'a spinster of fairly lowly background', hearing gossip that another woman was pregnant, upbraided the scandalmongers, declaring 'they might as well take her life as her good name from her'. On this he comments: 'It is instructive that a country girl in the north of England should express notions of honour identical to those held in the upper reaches of society.'

To take another example: in reading Le Roy Ladurie's *Montaillou*, were it not for Ladurie's anxious reminders that we are dealing with 'peasants', we might easily assume we were reading about aristocrats; this would be the natural inference to draw from so much reckless freedom of thought and behaviour, such respect for cour-

tesies and such emphasis upon honour. But though natural, it would
be wrong. There is no reason to suppose that codes of honour, and
preoccupation with 'face', on the part of the socially humble, are
imitated from the aristocracy; rather, aristocratic 'honour' is an ela-
boration of a common human concern.

I was exaggerating when I spoke of the pleasures of honour as
'universal'. For—and this is most important—there will be a few
individuals who are considered as having no honour, or anything
'due' to them at all; and such people will be thought of, precisely, as
socially non-existent. Though there again, it will be hard actually to
identify any such individuals, and it will be more that theory
requires their existence. What, rather, you may actually find in flesh
and blood is people, like beggars or professional thieves, who have
gone through a ritual of abjuring honour; and then honour promptly
slips in again at the back door, in the form of honour among thieves.
Honour is very pervasive, and one needs to look twice or thrice at
statements to the effect that anyone is 'without honour'. On the
other hand it is an essential feature of an honour-based community
that almost anyone, whatever his or her social circumstances, will
claim the luxury of vilifying a 'mob', 'rabble', or 'dregs of society'.*

I have been conflating two systems so far: one in which the monarch is the 'fountain of honour', that is to say is able to create
honour—so that his or her subjects grow ambitious to win specified
'honours'; and the other, in which the assertion or the defence of
one's honour is merely an ideal expression of one's relation to the
community at large. Nevertheless, one can regard both as, in a
sense, pleasure-systems—which attach a pleasure (known as 'pride')
to communal existence as well as a painful burden, the defending of
one's honour.

Honour-systems in their pure form will inevitably be extraverted
in character and lay their main stress on the visible signs of honour.
According to such codes, the great have a positive moral duty to
keep up their 'state' and outward show and should be rebuked when
they shirk it. (Mark Girouard, in his *Life in the English Country House*,
quotes the complaint of 'R. B.', author of *Some Rules and Orders for the
Government of an Earle* (*c.*1605): 'noble men in these days (for the most
part) like better to be served with pages and groomes, than in their
estate which belongeth to their degree.')[8]

* See Roget's *Thesaurus*, s.v. *Commonalty*: 'The mob, rabble, rabble-rout, *canaille*; the
scum or dregs of the people, or of society; *faex populi*; *profanum vulgus*; low company,
vermin, nobody.'

It is, however, common for honour-systems over the years, and in the name of 'civilization' and 'enlightenment', to be interiorized, and modified in the direction of modesty, reserve, exclusivity, and social invisibility. The movement will begin from the court or metropolis; and the purer forms of 'honour'-system will, in the eyes of the exponents of the new social doctrines, come to seem old-fashioned and quaint, not to say grotesquely narrow and philistine. Many are the jokes, and caricatures, and stage-types that will be based upon them; though none the less, they will prove to have a strong capacity for survival.

Yves Castan, in *Honnêteté et relations sociales en Languedoc 1715–1780* (1974), has given a striking account of the rigidly 'honour'-bound way of life still surviving in non-French-speaking Languedoc in the eighteenth century. His book is based on depositions and reports from the archives of the courts of Toulouse and its environs—the litigants in question being mainly non-French-speaking small farmers, craftsmen, shopkeepers and the like. Here is a series of remarks from it:

[*On honour*]

Law-suits are not provoked by sheer want. 'The litigation reflects, rather, an aspiration towards a status of independence, prestige, free movement, an aspiration sticking closely, as it must do, to models which it is deemed possible to imitate.' Law-suits give people the pleasure of feeling they have no superiors.

The debates about presumption of guilt that take place in the popular forum [*milieu populaire*] are dominated by references to honour . . . The formula which clinches the self-justifications of an accused or reproached witness is often: 'I have as much honour as him.' To be '*brave*'—the word is in frequent use in recognizances and formal 'compositions' [i.e. settlements of disputes]—does not mean assuming a facile *bonhomie*, nor laying claim to martial courage, it signifies a constant disposition to conduct oneself with honour. When this latter word [i.e. 'honour'] has acquired a special value as a term of social approval and it seems derisory to apply it to too humble a sort of person, the term '*brave*', a more familiar one and with a more strictly ethical signification, is preferred, since it asserts the same requirement of pride.

You abuse enemies or malefactors by accusing them of the crime they have *not* committed [i.e. you attack their honour and *status*]. Thus: 'You have killed me, you thief!' 'You have robbed me, you whore!'

[*On charity*]

General benevolence or charity are not demanded of people. You may leave a dying man unaided, having ascertained that he has no claim on you by reason of kinship, neighbourliness, or related interests. Real poverty is such a disgrace that it is not commented on in documents, and the term *gueux* [beggarly scoundrel] is not used, except in the case of wretches who 'can lay no claim to the defence of their own honour'. True poverty 'imposes a veritable internal exile'.

[*On virtue*]

The oven, the washing-place, the shop are the privileged scenes where women exchange information and unburden themselves of their quarrels, untroubled by the absurd niceties about honour which embarrass their husbands and brothers. The praises of good looks, health, 'race' and social superiorities are loudly sung; and harsh things are said about the physically handicapped, people with tarnished reputations, paupers, *les crie-famine*, the 'race of lackeys', and suffocators of bastards; here are commemorated generosities, mendicities, humiliations, and faults.

The virtues expected of a woman are not imposed on a man, but on the other hand he is not expected necessarily to define himself by opposition to those virtues. He can be a drunkard or a prodigal, or on the contrary chaste and provident, and both behaviours are acceptable. The temperamentally prudent man need not pretend to be more of a 'dog' than he is, so long as he does not show himself too worried about his own family's opinion.[9]

It is, as described by Castan, a very complete and coherent outlook; though of course by then to the Parisian and 'enlightened' French-speaking France generally it appeared intensely quaint. Somehow it strikes one as familiar. It puts me in mind of George Eliot's account of Maggie Tulliver's uncles and aunts, in *The Mill on the Floss*. These Dodson and Clegg relations of Maggie's—one of the uncles is a wool-stapler, one is a farmer, one becomes a manager in a large mill-owning and ship-owning business—tend not to think of themselves as 'gentry', nor indeed to think about the 'gentry' much at all, being themselves full of family pride. It does not make them socially envious when Mr Tulliver decides to make his son Tom into a 'gentleman', only angry at the foolhardy expense. Their pride is a matter of tradition.

There were particular ways of doing everything in that family: particular ways of bleaching the linen, of making the cowslip wine, curing the hams, and keeping the bottled gooseberries; so that no daughter of that house could be indifferent to the privilege of having been born a Dodson, rather than a Gibson or a Watson. Funerals were always conducted with peculiar propriety in the Dodson family: the hat-bands were never of a blue shade, the gloves never split at the thumb, everybody was a mourner who ought to be, and there were always scarfs for the bearers. When one of the family was in trouble or sickness, all the rest went to visit the unfortunate member, usually at the same time, and did not shrink from uttering the most disagreeable truths that correct family feeling dictated . . . There were some Dodsons less like the family than others—that was admitted; but in so far as they were 'kin', they were of necessity better than those who were no 'kin' . . . [Mrs Tulliver] was thankful to have been a Dodson, and to have one child who took after her own family, at least in his features and complexion, in liking salt and in eating beans, which a Tulliver never did.[10]

On doctors, the Dodson view is that it is not respectable to 'play with your own inside' when you have money to pay for a doctor. On mourning: Mrs Clegg 'always cried just as much as was proper when anything happened to her own "kin", but not on other occasions'. On physical handicap: in the eyes of the Dodsons the hump-backed Philip Wakem is, disapprovingly, 'That mis-made son o' Lawyer Wakem's'. On money:

To be honest and poor was never a Dodson motto, still less to seem rich though being poor; rather, the family badge was to be honest and rich; and not only rich, but richer than was supposed. To live respected and have the proper bearers at your funeral, was an achievement of the ends of existence that would be entirely nullified if, on the reading of your Will, you sank in the opinion of your fellow-men, either by turning out to be poorer than they expected, or by leaving your money in a capricious manner, without strict regard to degree of kin.[11]

There seem to be some obvious likenesses here between the Dodson culture and that of Castan's Languedocians: the all-importance of pride, the restriction of philanthropy to one's kin, the scorn of poverty and physical handicap. Of course, the differences are also great. Possessions loom much larger for the Dodsons and Cleggs, who are indeed possession-mad; and 'respectability' and regard for neighbourhood opinion has a somewhat different ring for them. Nevertheless theirs is still unmistakably an 'honour'-system. But what one also notices in their outlook and in that of the Languedocians is certain parallels with the aristocratic outlook. Dodson family pride, the theory of an intrinsic and mystic Dodson superiority, evinced in hereditary traits like a taste for salt: it is not too easy, really, to distinguish this from the lordly pride of Talbots and Beauchamps—the pride of 'birth', blue blood and Norman profiles.

Let us now turn to the long process of interiorization by which, to the 'enlightened' of Diderot's France, the codes of Castan's provincials have become a grotesque anachronism, the development by which the Dodson and Clegg outlook, so familiar to the young Marian Evans, has become so infinitely alien to the nineteenth-century intellectual 'George Eliot'. It is a process by which 'honour' is given a more inward and ethical flavour and by which the pleasures of 'outward' honour are subjected to restraint, so that henceforth they have to be enjoyed to some extent secretly. Such a development took place both in England and France (of course not only there), and a point to make about it right away is that, socially speaking, it had, and was bound to have, a *separating* tendency. In a community run according to outward honour it would presumably be the wish of its members to find as many opportunities as possible of advertising their honour. Thus 'honour' would be socially cohesive: no use in enjoying honour on your own. When, however, 'honour' becomes interiorized, there comes to be less need for an audience, and correspondingly a certain attraction in reserving your lustre for those who can appreciate it—in becoming morally, or even physically, invisible to others.

In the remainder of this chapter I shall deal with the 'interiorizing' of honour in the form which it had taken in France. (It took a somewhat different form in England, and I shall come to that in the next chapter, on 'The Gentleman'.)

The *honnête homme*

A notable example of the modifying of 'honour' was the cult of *honnêteté* and the *honnête homme* which swept France, or at any rate Paris, in the mid-seventeenth century. Its purpose, as I have said, was to provide a more 'inward' alternative to the old-fashioned man of honour or *homme d'honneur*—the rigid stickler for visible honour, precedence and the 'point of honour'. There were a number of versions of *honnêteté*, ranging from the completest man-of-the-worldliness to austere Pascalian spirituality,[12] and I will merely jot down a few leading traits. The *honnête homme* was to please, to be 'winning'. He was to be easy, flexible and unpedantic and disinclined to take offence over trifles. He was to be alert and subtle, concealing his real thoughts under a mask of amenity. And these qualities were to be acquired by strenuous self-cultivation and a Stoic steeling of the soul against untidy passions, combined with an unbought grace, a *je ne sais quoi*, which was the secular equivalent of divine grace. *Honnêteté* was conceived in some sense in opposition to the court and to 'feudal' notions of nobility. It was a system of conduct claiming to transcend considerations of rank and promoting an egalitarian free-masonry of *honnêtes gens*. Thus the members of the Rambouillet and Scudéry *salons* were rebaptized with pseudo-classical names, thereby losing their distinguishing 'de'—much as Molière's aristocratic characters have socially neutral names like Alceste or Philinthe. From this point of view, *honnêteté* is designed as a justification or *apologia* for privilege.

'Honour', at whatever level of society, is a matter of exacting or granting what is due to oneself or others in the way of respect, courtesy, or ceremony and may be quite brutal in its assertion of social differences. *Honnêteté*, by contrast, prescribes that everyone (or almost everyone) should be granted the same outward cour-tesy. 'The courtier, and after him the Parisian, were possessed by the idea that the forms of politeness were merely "small change", to be distributed without stint since they were without solid worth, if not without effect. One could refuse them only to social pests and trouble-makers who abused the convention.'[13] This is, of course, the most prevalent Western notion of 'politeness' even today.

One can think of *honnêteté* as a system adapted to Paris, where a man-of-the-world would be meeting people whose social pretensions he did not know and could not be blamed for not knowing (though indeed the *honnête homme* would not identify with the court or even the metropolis but would think of himself as belonging to the *grand monde* or 'great world'). Being thus accustomed to meet strangers, he would need to know how to put out social feelers or take sound-ings—meanwhile maintaining a front of perfect amenity. *Honnêteté*'s view, one hardly known to medieval or Renaissance courtesy, was that a 'true' gentleman or lady conceals the social judgements he or she is passing. Nothing could be more *malhonnête* than the awful can-dour of the medieval Countess to her plebeian suitor in Andreas Capellanus's *Art of Courtly Love*—explaining to him that mere good character without rank can hardly be expected to win her hand, and complaining that, unlike the appearance of the truly knightly, 'your calves are fat and roundly turned, ending abruptly, and your feet are huge and immensely spread out so that they are as broad as they are long'.[14]

Compared with antique 'honour', the doctrine of *honnêteté* was, as we have seen, a 'modesty'. The point is made clear in Lord Chester-field's *Letters to his Son*, which explicitly inculcate French manners, *honnête* manners, rather than English.* It is proper to shine in one's dress, Chesterfield tells his son, but it must be in the modern way: not by 'a clumsy load of gold and silver, but by the taste and fashion of it'.[15] As for conversation, one should take great care not to shine too much in it, for no one will thank you for doing so. Parodying St Paul, he preaches: 'one must . . . become all things to all men, to gain some.'[16]

Nevertheless the *honnête* code (by this time a somewhat tired commonplace in France) struck the English as immodest—as altogether too Frenchified and biased towards outwards show. Dr Johnson's fulminations against Chesterfield's Letters ('they teach the morals of a whore, and the manners of a dancing-master') are well known and significant. 'Honour' in England had taken a somewhat different course, and to follow its vicissitudes we shall need to trace the history of 'the gentleman'.

---

* 'Your exercises of riding, fencing, and dancing, will civilise and fashion your body and your limbs, and give you, if you will but take it, *l'air d'un honnête homme*' (Chesterfield, *Letters to his Son*: 21 June 1748).

8

The 'gentleman'

Why the modification of 'honour' took a different course in England from what it did in France seems to relate to a significant divergence that took place in the late Middle Ages between England and the rest of Europe—I mean, the creation in England of a distinction (unknown to the rest of Europe) between a 'nobleman' and a 'gentleman'. The story may be said to begin in the fifteenth century, with the formation of an English peerage. This was an innovation; hereditary rank was not characteristic of the earlier Middle Ages, and as late as 1300 there was only one heritable rank in England, that of earl (nor had this always been hereditary). Some time in the 1400s, however, there began to be drawn a dividing-line between 'lords' (temporal and spiritual) and the rest of armigerous society; and hand-in-hand with this there began to be devised a clear-cut system of hereditary and ornamental 'ranks'. (By 1500 there were five of them: duke, marquis, earl, viscount, baron.) This segregating of a very small body of 'lords' from the rest of the English nobility and gentry, and the bestowing on it of legal privileges, was a notable step, setting England on a path different from France (where *noble* and *gentilhomme*, nobility and gentry, have remained synonymous terms).[1] It went, moreover, with a general sorting-out of social categories and descriptions. A Statute of 1413 laid it down that in writs and appeals concerning personal actions, the defendant's place of residence and his 'estate degree of mystery' should be stated; and the practice soon spread to other types of legal document.[2]

It was in these circumstances that there was born the concept of the 'gentleman'. Up to now the word had, in a vague way, designated 'knights' and freemen generally; but now that 'lord' had become a status, there was use for a contradistinguishing status, 'gentleman'— signifying 'a highly respectable person, *not* a lord'. It was not, at its origin, a very glamorous status-name. As K. B. McFarlane has written: 'The gentry did not so much rise (though some did) during the later middle ages as fall from the nobility which their antecessors had enjoyed in common with all landowners . . . '.[3] A claim to gentility might rest on various different bases. It might be a pretension founded on a newly acquired fortune, or again it might derive from a post in a noble or royal household, or from military rank. It was in many cases a reflected or derivative dignity, its sense being that one was 'somebody's gentleman', a satellite of a great man.

It may be noticed that 'gentleman', and equally 'lord', are just what the term 'social status' seems best fitted to denote: i.e. a named position of honour or esteem, *not* defined by titular rank. ('Lord'—as opposed to 'viscount' or 'marquis'—is not the name of a rank.) There have, in fact, been rather few such social-status names, but another important one is 'yeoman'. It seems to have arisen at roughly the same period, and indeed its history shows a certain resemblance to that of the 'gentleman'. In the early fifteenth century the dominant sense of 'yeoman' was still that of *somebody*'s yeoman, an attendant or henchman—as in Chaucer's Yeoman (a forester attendant upon the Squire) and his Canon's Yeoman (a front-man to a shady operator). It also carried in certain contexts an association with inferiority, so that in merchant companies those outside the *élite* of liverymen were known as 'yeomen'. As time went on, 'gentleman' and 'yeoman' entered into a curious alliance, and, shedding their 'dependent' associations, they succeeded in hoisting each other up in social and ideological prestige. Thus, it became convenient for the Tudor establishment to invoke a race of sturdy English 'yeomen'—reliable, substantial rural types who (allegedly) had a long-standing and close relationship with the gentry and nobility and, in consort with them, made up a team which was the envy and despair of other nations. Sir Thomas Smith, in his *De republica Anglorum* (written, appropriately, in France) gave a celebrated eulogy of this supposed partnership:

These [yeomen] are they which in the old world gat that honour to Englande, not that either for witte, conduction, or for power they are or were ever to be compared to the gentleman, but because they be so manie in number, so obedient at the Lordes call. . . . These were the good archers in times past, and that stable troupe of footemen that affaide all France, that would rather die all, than once abandon the knight or gentleman their Captain . . . who at those daies commonly was their Lorde, and whose tenaunts they were . . . [4]

This same myth of partnership, though not under the same nomenclature, was still influential right up to the First World War.*

* It is according to a somewhat similar pattern that the 'Squire' or 'Esquire', subject over the centuries to various half-conflicting chivalric, 'service', and quasi-legal definitions, ripens in the eighteenth century into the 'country squire'—twin prop, with the parson, of an idealized 'social order'.

By the early seventeenth century the name of 'gentleman' had acquired much kudos, and not only among Cavaliers. It had become a name to be coveted and to be defended against challenge; and indeed during the 1630s people would bring actions in the Earl Marshal's court to vindicate their right to it. Nothing could better bring home to us how the concept functioned. The facts adduced in this court to prove a right to the name 'gentleman' were, according to G. D. Squibb, 'many and varied'.[5] It might be a certificate that one was related to an earl, or the fact that one had held a military commission, or that one had previously figured in a legal document with the addition 'Gentleman', or that one's father had been a justice of the peace or had been to Oxford. To the accusation that one was in 'trade', and therefore could not be a gentleman, there was a whole range of possible answers. One plaintiff before the court deposed that he was a 'gentleman by birth and linen draper by trade'; another that, though he had sometimes worked at the forge and anvil, he had never been seen to wear a leather apron. That one possessed a coat of arms could be a strong argument, but the court ruled (in *Stepkin v. Dobbins* 1638) that a man could be a gentleman even if not entitled to arms.

By such pliable methods was the argument about gentility conducted at the mundane and legal level. It should be remembered, too, that a very cool usage of the term 'gentleman', as meaning simply *looking* like a gentleman, existed comfortably side-by-side with more ambitious ones. It is the one enunciated by Robinson Crusoe:

It was my great misfortune, that in all these adventures I did not ship myself as a sailor; whereby, though I might indeed have worked a little harder than ordinary, yet, at the same time, I had learned the duty and office of a foremastman, and in time might have qualified myself for a mate or lieutenant, if not a master: but as it was always my fate to choose for the worse, so I did here; for having money in my pocket, and good clothes upon my back, I would always go on board in the habit of a gentleman . . .[6]

At the ethical level, meanwhile, the question who *was* a gentleman was by tacit agreement sidestepped. By a characteristic move, the courtesy-books of the seventeenth century deliberately equated gentility and nobility. Thus the title-page of Henry Peacham's *Compleat Gentleman* (1622) speaks of the 'Commendable Qualities concerning Minde or Bodie that may be required in a Noble Gentleman'. (Spenser, more ambiguously, declared it his aim in *The Faerie Queene*

'to fashion a gentleman or noble person in virtuous discipline'.)
Such books as Peacham's or as Richard Braithwait's *The English
Gentleman* (1630)—works no doubt partly aimed at tutors—were not
essentially polemical at all; their complaints that the 'unworthy'
were buying themselves patents of gentility had no political edge
and were no more than common form.

One can see why the concept 'gentleman', and its partner 'yeoman', had such a successful career. These relate partly to the nature
of a 'social status' and the difference between a social status and a
'rank'. The social status of 'gentleman' gains its suggestive force,
and its enormous potential for rhetorical and ideological exploitation, from its vagueness and lack of semantic anchorage. It has
ranking implication—for one of the subsidiary connotations of 'yeoman' is 'non-gentleman'—yet it is not a rank and has no such fixed
field of reference as a rank. (One is not a 'gentleman' in the uncon-
tentious way that one is a viscount or a colonel or an Under-
Secretary.) Again, it carries a claim to ethical qualities, yet its leading meaning (or as you might say, its meaning of last resort) refers to
outward social position and dignity; and the etymologies for it
('gens', 'Gentile' etc.) have to do with the worldly and the external.

This equivocation between the ethical and the social proved very
fruitful and indeed historically important. 'Gentlemanliness' in due
course came to be a reproof to overbearing (or debauched, or swag-
gering) 'lordly' ways, and it was dinned into the ears of aristocrats
that 'lords' have a duty, which they do not always live up to, to be
'gentlemen'. The development seems to go hand-in-hand with the
change noticed by William Empson in regard to the word 'honest'.
In all Romance languages apart from English 'honest' is synonymous with 'honourable' and carries with it the full range of connotations of 'honour', including worldly dignity and display. In
England, however, some time in the sixteenth century, the word
'honest' split away from the word 'honourable', taking as its new
head-meaning the 'modest' virtues of 'not lying, not stealing, keeping promises' (though retaining 'outward honour' connotations
among its subsidiary meanings).[7] It thus became a richly ambiguous word, full of rhetorical potentialities. By means of it, as Empson
shows, all sorts of sectional interests, in due course, found themselves able to lay claim to ethical approval, without renouncing their
claim to worldly and social approval. 'Honest' could be used, variously, for teasing the Puritans (they were not 'honest good fellows'),
for justifying libertinism (rakes were at least 'honest' with

themselves), for making fun of a barbarous aristocracy (by making their boon-companion use of the term 'honest' appear 'low'), for taking down the pride of statesmen (by equating them with 'honest' tradesmen and 'honest' highwaymen), and for patronizing the socially underprivileged ('honest Jones, our butcher'). The word 'honesty' made much capital out of its unpretentiousness, though still slyly reminding hearers of its noble and worldly honourable ancestry. 'Honest' (so much more downright in its implications than the French *honnête*), in partnership with 'gentleman' (so much less bald an assertion of social privilege than the French *gentilhomme*), did something to help save the English nobility from the guillotine.

From the eighteenth century onwards debates about social ethics in England tended increasingly to turn on the definition, or re-definition, of the 'gentleman'. Steele, in the *Guardian*, proposed a reformist definition of the 'gentleman', as a corrective to the Restoration bully and rake.

When I consider the frame of mind peculiar to a gentleman, I suppose it is graced with all the dignity and elevation of spirit that human nature is capable of. To this I would have joined a clear understanding, a reason free from prejudice, a steady judgement, and an extensive knowledge. When I think of the heart of a gentleman, I imagine it firm and intrepid, void of all inordinate passions, and full of tenderness, compassion and benevolence. When I view the fine gentleman with regard to his manners, methinks I see him modest without bashfulness, frank and affable without impertinence, obliging and complaisant without servility, cheerful and in good humour without noise.[8]

Robin Gilmour says of this, in *The Idea of the Gentleman in the Victorian Novel* (1981), that

the challenge lies in its very moderation and restraint . . . it becomes part of a brilliant campaign to replace the gentleman of tradition—the rake, the beau, the bucolic Tory squire, the duelling man of 'honour'—with a more sober and domesticated type, suitable to a society that was emerging from the violence of civil war and foreign conquest and coming to terms with its destiny as a trading nation.[9]

Actually, though, I think I would gloss the matter rather differently. For after all, when Addison and Steele were writing, the Civil Wars, and even the Restoration rakehells, were well in the past. The present threat was a rather different one: it was that the 'great' were growing steadily greater, as well as more numerous. Vast Palladian palaces (so many Versailles) were rising in the shires, and their owners were commissioning overweening funeral monuments, from which all pretence of religious humility had been banished. It was the age of 'greatness', of monarchs nicknamed 'The Great' and of Thomas Gray's 'proud'—those for whom 'The pealing anthem swells the note of praise.'

Against this 'greatness', the concept of the 'gentleman' provided a certain protection. Fielding, for instance, was deliberately defensive towards the 'great', not only in his satire on highwayman-like 'greatness' in *Jonathan Wild the Great* but also in his fondness for little and commonplace heroes and heroines, like Tom, Sophia, and Captain Booth.* It was what you might call a 'modesty'. We find even more emphasis on it later, in Jane Austen. The picture that Jane Austen projects of her 'Hartfield' and 'Longbourn' gentry is of people with no lust for 'great' connections; the idea of dukes and magnates is to be held at a distance, a distancing as important as her more commented-upon silence upon servants, upon 'guilt and misery', and upon the Napoleonic Wars. 'Littleness' seems indeed a ruling principle in her novels, assuming as they do a code of conduct which restricts the characters to the smaller gestures.

It was perhaps for similar or related motives that Fielding, as William Empson has pointed out, adopted a 'roughness' ploy—i.e. a disguising of one's gentility under roughness, rudeness, shabbiness or illiteracy.

What people found so entertaining at the time, when Fielding attacked Richardson in a rather explosive class situation (the eager readers of Richardson in French were presumably heading towards the French Revolution), was that the classes seemed to have swappped over. The printer's apprentice was the gentlemanly expert on manners, indeed the first English writer to be accepted as one by the polite French; whereas if you went to Fielding, they liked to say at the time, you would find him drunk in bed with his cook and still boasting he was related to the Hapsburgs. His answer to Richardson was thus: 'But I know what a gentleman is: I am one.' . . . He provided a new idea of the aristocrat, with the added claim that it was an older tradition; and he did seem to clear the subject up rather—you could hardly deny that he was a better idea than Lord Chesterfield.[10]

What comes home to us, though, is that Fielding's defensiveness

---

* One thinks, too, of Squire Western on 'lords': 'It is true indeed, there be larger estates in the kingdom, but not in this county, and I had rather bate something, than marry my daughter among strangers and foreigners. Besides most o' zuch great estates be in the hands of the lords, and I heate the very name of *themmun*.'

(*Tom Jones*, Book 6, chapter 2)

worked downwards as well as upwards. If it was aimed against the
'great' it was also aimed against the 'low' and against social inter-
lopers. His position on the 'gentleman' question was not in the least
egalitarian or, in that sense, reformist. On the contrary, it was
rigidly 'predestinarian'. The trouble with the rascally Ensign North-
erton, according to Fielding, is simply that he was not a gentleman.
The judgement 'no-gentleman' is passed on him on inward, and for
that reason all the more inflexible, grounds.

> And here, reader, we must strictly caution thee, that thou does not take any
> occasion from the misbehaviour of such a wretch as this, to reflect on so
> worthy and honourable a body of men, as are the officers of our army in
> general. Thou wilt be pleased to consider, that this fellow, as we have
> already informed thee, had neither the birth nor education of a gentleman,
> nor was a proper person to be enrolled among the number of such.[11]

'The gentleman' and 'class'

With the nineteenth century and the coming of 'class', a new question presents itself: what is the relationship of the concept of 'the
gentleman' to the concept of 'class'? It cannot help striking us rather
forcefully that the rise of 'class' in the 1830s did not coincide with the
decline of the 'gentleman'. On the contrary the mid-Victorian
period was the very heyday and apogee of 'the gentleman', in the
sense that the term seemed at this time to be on everyone's mind and
tongue. It was in the years 1840–80, writes Robin Gilmour, that 'the
nature of gentlemanliness was more anxiously debated and more
variously defined than at any time before or since'.[12] These years
were to witness the Kenelm Digby medieval-revival version of the
'gentleman', with its emphasis on Christian chivalry; the Charles
Kingsley version, with its emphasis on 'manliness'; the Thomas
Arnold version, with its stress on earnestness; the nostalgic-
Quixotic, or 'last of the gentlemen', version of Thackeray;
Newman's cunning counterblast to Digby, the gentleman as virtuous pagan; and Trollope's extensive gallery of portraits of 'true
gentlemen' and 'perfect gentlemen' (their gentlemanliness turning
especially on attitudes towards money).

Now, 'gentlemanliness' is a binary scheme (gentleman/not gentleman), whereas 'class', in its English version, is a tripartite one
(upper/middle/lower). Thus the two systems are plainly in conflict,
and in their conflict they provided large scope for manœuvre, of the
kind this book has so often discussed.

'Class', in its early days, fought an uphill battle against the 'gentleman'. James Mill, as we saw, strove hard to attach kudos to the idea of a 'middle class'; his efforts, however, had no lasting success. Thus the tone in which the 'middle class' or 'middle classes' are referred to in the mid-Victorian period seems almost invariably to be, in some degree, contemptuous or defensive. It is contemptuous, for instance, in George Eliot's *Felix Holt*, both on the part of the 'gentlemanly' Harold Transom and of the working man Felix (and indeed of George Eliot herself, as narrator). For Transom the implication of 'middle class' is explicitly 'not a gentleman or lady, whatever else they may be'; and he describes the lawyer Jermyn (who ironically later turns out to be his own father) as 'one of your middle-class upstarts who want to rank with gentlemen, and think they'll do it with kid gloves and new furniture'.[13] Felix Holt is equally dismissive: 'Why should I want to get into the middle class because I have some learning? . . . I'll have none of your clerkly gentility.'[14] With Matthew Arnold and Cobden, as we saw, the attitude was contemptuous-defensive: that is to say they were ready to claim membership of the 'middle class', for certain polemical purposes, yet be abusive about it too. The same classic manœuvre is found in Bagehot when, in *The English Constitution* (1867), he paints the 'middle classes' as the effective rulers of Britain, and the aristocracy as its 'spectacle' or 'theatre', yet makes it firmly, if tacitly, plain that he exempts himself from the 'middle classes'.

The middle classes—the ordinary majority of educated men—are in the present day the despotic power in England. 'Public opinion', nowadays, 'is the opinion of the bald-headed man at the back of the omnibus.' It is *not* the opinion of the aristocratical classes as such; or of the most educated or refined classes as such; it is simply the opinion of the ordinary mass of educated, but still commonplace mankind.[15]

Bagehot here observes a law I have mentioned before: when in difficulties, create another class. To give oneself an acceptable station (for he would not claim to be 'aristocratical') he invents a group called 'the most educated or refined classes'. Finally, to complete our inventory of ploys, we see Anthony Trollope, in his novels, deliberately boycotting the notion of 'class' as a false modern invention, and offering in its place a revised and reformist theory of 'the gentleman'. None of the great Victorian novelists, indeed, talk *much* about 'class', a fact which connects with their habit of setting their novels back in time.

The social shibboleth

It is borne in on us how important the period of the 1830s (the formative period of the Victorian novelists) is for our whole subject. In a way, it is not too easy to look back behind it, since notions and categories acquired then condition our vision. According to observers like Carlyle, Thackeray, and Lytton, the period saw a sudden nationwide epidemic of social striving and of scrambling for 'gentility'; and though we need not adopt their apocalyptic tone, it seems plain that—at the 'purely social' level, as well as so many others—a large upheaval was in fact taking place.

It was much about this period that the 'social shibboleth' came into its own—I mean, the theory that social origin can be inferred from certain small indicators. This was natural, for evidently, when 'honour' is no longer to be outwardly asserted but adopts disguises, there will be a need for a corresponding technique for detecting it (or its lack). Thus it was at this moment that certain famous and classic shibboleths were institutionalized.

The so-called 'dropped *h*' was one of these, indeed you might say it became *the* archetypical social shibboleth, and it is worth briefly tracing how *h*-dropping acquired its symbolic status. The duty set itself by the Augustan age was to 'correct' and refine the English tongue; and this meant, so far as pronunciation is concerned, the privileging of an artificial and ideal metropolitan accent as against all regional ones. Now, as will be seen, this put Cockney, the dialect of the humbler inhabitants of the metropolis, in a special position. If regional dialects were to be 'corrected', this was the one nearest to hand, the one most continually in the ear of the 'polite' speaker, and accordingly the one most likely to figure as the archetype of 'incorrectness'.* It was only a short step from this to selecting some feature of Cockney as a shibboleth distinguishing the gentleman from the non-gentleman.

It remains to explain why *h* should have been the chosen feature. In the many discussions of Cockney in the late eighteenth and early

---

* John Walker, in his *Critical Pronouncing Dictionary*, first published in 1791, gives 'Rules to be observed by the natives of Scotland, Ireland, and London, for avoiding their respective peculiarities'. He puts the point very clearly: 'though the inhabitants of London have this manifest advantage over all the other inhabitants of the island, they have the disadvantage of being more disgraced by their peculiarities than any other people . . . Hence it is, that the vulgar pronunciation of London, though not half so erroneous as that of Scotland, Ireland, or any of the provinces, is, to a person of correct taste, a thousand times more offensive and disgusting.'

nineteenth century, the Cockney handling of *h* was not much remarked upon, the feature drawing most attention, so far as pronunciation is concerned, being what we think of as 'Weller-ism', i.e. its handling of *v* and *w*. Why, then, was *h* felt to be the most effective shibboleth? The answer seems to be that for a very long time the status of *h* had been unstable in English.[16] For several centuries after the Conquest, except in certain limited areas, the sounded initial *h* seems to have dropped out of English, as it had done in French and Italian; and though it gradually returned, practice was for long very variable (as may be seen from the punning on 'hair' and 'air' etc., in Elizabethan writers). Thus what we have in *h* is something rather akin to what we have found in 'class' and 'the gentleman', i.e. an area of ambiguity or uncertainty, eminently suitable for exploitation for social propaganda. The thought 'Only the socially superior know how to behave in the difficult matter of the *h*' leads naturally into 'Let this, the sounding or not sounding of *h* in certain words, be a test determining who is a gentleman and who is not.' It also leads, equally naturally, into speaking of '*dropping* aitches'. It is not quite plain that Cockney was entirely *h*-less; more likely it had its own regional set of rules as to which words should have their *h* sounded and which not.[17] However, if you call it 'dropping of aitches', it becomes easier—this is a familiar innuendo in *Punch* jokes—to explain the putting in of aitches in the 'wrong' place as a vain attempt to ape gentlemanly ways. By 1870 we find Dean Alford complaining of the extreme hideousness and 'offensiveness' of the 'dropped aitch', stoutly denying that there was ever any uncertainty, among the educated, as to when to sound the *h*, and—most significant of all—dissociating the 'dropped *h*' from Cockney and giving it the character of a general fault or social crime.

This is a vulgarism not confined to this or that province of England, nor especially prevalent in one county or another, but incident throughout England to persons of low breeding and inferior education, principally to those amongst the inhabitants of towns.[18]

The 'non-gentleman'

What seems to run through the matters we have been discussing—the rivalry between the 'class'-system of thought and the 'gentleman-versus-non-gentleman' one, and the rise of the social 'shibboleth'—is the note of the *negative*. Robin Gilmour explains the debate about the 'gentleman' in the Victorian period, and Victorian efforts to 'moralise' gentlemanliness, as an attempt to 'redefine the idea of the gentleman to fit a middle class rather than an aristocratic context'.[19] This explanation goes a certain way, but what it seems to me to miss is the strongly negative note of Victorian thought on 'the gentleman'.

The simple interpretation of the various accounts of the 'gentleman' is that they were offered as models. I think, though, that this is to misunderstand them. It was characteristic of the Victorian age that etiquette-books, books to teach you how to be a gentleman or a lady, were published in abundance but, by the 'superior', were treated with great scorn. It had not been so in the previous century. A book such as *The Man of Manners: or Plebeian Polished*, published in the 1730s, would not, one feels, have automatically provoked a sneer. Again, Richardson's novels were avowedly instructional and were intended to give guidance on 'how to think and act justly and prudently in the common Concerns of Human Life'. It would not have been alien to Richardson to give instruction on how to be a gentleman: and indeed to some extent in *Sir Charles Grandison*, this is what he is doing.

What the Victorian sneer at social self-help conveys is the doctrine I have called 'social predestinarianism', the theory that you have already to be a gentleman before you can begin to act like one or even to know what gentlemanliness means. Gentlemanliness, according to this view, is a state of grace, unattainable by human effort: you either have it or you don't. Thus the novels of Thackeray and Meredith and Trollope, which attach such importance to the 'gentleman', are not really instructional or model-giving. They are, rather, from this point of view, pure romances—romances about the ineffable and unlearnable state of grace known as 'being a gentleman'.

Or we may put the matter in a different way. They offer a model, but it is of a purely negative kind. Deliberately elusive and self-contradictory about 'how to be a gentleman', they are practical and explicit about how *not* to be one. This is where the narrator comes out to meet the reader; indeed it is the true, though concealed, *raison d'être* of the whole novelistic enterprise. The point is particularly clear with Trollope. He amuses himself by floating conflicting theories of the 'gentleman'. According to one of these Bertie Stanhope and his family are gentlemen and ladies. (Indeed, *of course*, they are gentlemen and ladies, in a certain basic sense that Trollope expects his reader to endorse.) According to another of his theories, however, they are after all *not* gentlemen and ladies—because they have no heart. There is an element of game in this mystification of Trollope's, and quite a stimulating game. But when it comes to Mr Slope in *Barchester Towers*, or Mr Bott in *Can you Forgive Her?*, games are laid aside. The judgement is firm, practical, and without redress. They are simply *not* gentlemen.

In a curious and in some ways impressive book, *The Gentleman in Trollope* (1982), Shirley Letwin makes out a case for Trollope as spokesman for—no less—an alternative to the whole Platonic-Augustinian-Thomistic-Kantian-Marxist-Freudian ethic of the 'Self-Divided Man'. This alternative morality of Trollope is, according to her, what defines the 'gentleman'; and to explain the morality of the gentleman, it is necessary—much more than with other moralities—to study it at work, and over a long period. She might, so she says, have taken her experimental examples from real life. However, it is more convenient to take them from Trollope's novels; and accordingly she takes us through all of Trollope's most famous 'gentlemen', eliciting to her own satisfaction at least, a coherent ethical system from their wildly various behaviour.

What Shirley Letwin is doing, it will be seen, is to treat Trollope's novels as courtesy-books; and this, to my mind, is actually to misunderstand them. Trollope's habitual answer, when asked to define a 'gentleman', was that it was a 'thing so impossible of definition and so capable of recognition'. In his *Autobiography* he says that, as what he is now writing will not be read till after his death, he will dare to assert that 'There are places in life which can hardly be well filled except by "Gentlemen".'

Were I to make such an assertion with reference to the House of Commons, nothing that I ever said again would receive the slightest attention. A man in public life could not do himself a greater injury than by saying in public that commissions in the army or navy, or berths in the Civil Service, should be given exclusively to gentlemen. He would be defied to define the term—and would fail should he attempt to do so. But he would know what he meant, and so very probably would they who defied him.[20]

Now, this proposition that, at heart, everybody knows a gentleman when they see one, agrees very badly with Trollope's own novels, which tend to take the form of a suspense-story on this very issue and to tease us with the question, 'Is so-and-so a gentleman?' (Of course we know he is a gentleman in a certain sense, but is he *really* a gentleman?) We have here a basic rhetorical ploy, of great importance in nineteenth-century Britain. The sentence 'Everybody, at heart, knows what a gentleman is and can recognize one' can even at the very best only mean 'Every *gentleman*, at heart, knows what a gentleman is and can recognize one'—a non-gentleman can scarcely be expected to know anything about the matter. But in the light of Trollope's novels, how we have really to read it is, I think, rather different. It is: 'It may not always be clear who is a gentleman, but one thing every gentleman *does* know—he knows when somebody is *not* a gentleman.'

Robin Gilmour, though he takes Thackeray and Trollope too much on trust for my liking, puts the point well when he writes, apropos of Dickens: 'Seeing gentlemen from the outside he came to appreciate both the centrality of the gentlemanly idea in Victorian culture and its underlying irony, that however earnestly it might be moralised, the concept depended for its existence upon exclusion, on separating gentlemen from non-gentlemen.'[21] Much comes to a focus in that 'irony', if irony is the word. As I said earlier, the Victorian novelists talk rather infrequently about 'class' and find themselves much more at home with the concept of 'the gentleman'. But in qualification of this, it has to be said their handling of 'the gentleman' represents, historically speaking, an almost complete reversal. In *Twelfth Night*, to Olivia's question 'What is your parentage?', 'Cesario' answers: 'Above my fortune, yet my state is well:/I am a gentleman', and what he (she) is asserting here is a modest and positive claim. By contrast, when 'gentlemanliness' figures centrally in a Victorian novel, its function, despite all appearances, is largely negative. That the almost destitute 'perpetual curate' Mr Crawley and the Duke of Omnium are both 'gentlemen' is the romance message of Trollope's novel; but on the contrary the realistic message of 'gentlemanliness' is that it gives, or seems to give, the right to *exclude*—to dismiss fellow-mortals as 'non-gentlemen'. By the time of Trollope the 'gentleman' concept, though never more prized, has become a system for ruling-out—in which it resembles 'class', which is purely a matter of separation and affirms no positive values at all. Thus the concepts of 'class' and of 'the gentleman' have revealed themselves as sisters under the skin.

*

9

Nietzsche revised

Let us consider the familiar fact that much of our ethical vocabulary, that is to say of our terms of moral praise and blame, derives from social position. Thus we have 'gentle', 'generous', 'honest', 'honourable', 'courteous', 'noble', 'well-bred', 'liberal'; and 'base', 'vile', 'villain', 'boor', 'churlish', 'mean', 'clown', 'degraded'—all of which, though we could hardly get on without them as praise-words or blame-words, refer by origin to social privilege or medieval legal status. The thought is a little embarrassing. And the first explanation that springs to mind is naturally in terms of social oppression. This, we are tempted to say, is the vocabulary of an oppressor group and has been formed on the principle that praiseworthiness is purely and simply—there is nothing more to it—a matter of belonging to that group, and blameworthiness of not belonging to it.

The most impressive version of this theory is Nietzsche's in *The Genealogy of Morals*. Nietzsche argues that the very idea of 'good' derives from the conqueror mentality; it does not refer to good *effects*, as felt by those to whom good is done, but springs rather from aristocratic self-approval.

Much rather has it been the good themselves, that is, the aristocratic, the powerful, the high-stationed, the high minded, who have felt that they themselves were good, that is to say of the first order, in contradistinction to all the low, the low minded, the vulgar, and the plebeian. It was out of this pathos of distance that they first arrogated the right to create values for their own profit, and to coin the names of such values . . . [1]

The notion of 'good' having originated in this way, it follows, (so runs Nietzsche's theory) that it has generated not one opposite but two—the notion of 'bad', which is a mere negative of 'good', adding nothing to the original concept: and the notion of 'evil', which is the fruit of the 'slave-revolt in morals', embodying a deeply contrived revenge on the part of the underprivileged.

The revolt of the slaves in morals begins in the very principle of *resentment* becoming creative and giving birth to values—a resentment experienced by creatures who, deprived as they are of the proper outlet of action, are forced to find their compensation in an imaginary revenge. While every aristocratic morality springs from a triumphant affirmation of its own demands, the slave morality says 'no' from the very outset to what is 'outside itself', 'different from itself', and 'not itself': and this 'no' is its creative deed. This volte-face of the valuing standpoint—this *inevitable* gravitation to the objective instead of back to the subjective—is typical of 'resentment': the slave morality requires as the condition of its existence an external and objective world, to employ physiological terminology, it requires objective stimuli to be capable of action at all—its action is fundamentally a reaction.

The contrary is the case when we come to the aristocrat's system of values: it acts and grows spontaneously, it merely seeks its antithesis in order to pronounce a more grateful and exultant 'yes' to its own self;—its negative conception, 'low', 'vulgar', 'bad' is merely a pale late-born foil in comparison with its positive and fundamental conception (saturated as it is with life and passion), of 'we aristocrats, we good ones, we beautiful ones, we happy ones'.[2]

As a historical myth, this is better than most, and indeed it is a work of genius. And since it is a myth, various literal-minded objections to it must fall down. It is no real criticism of Nietzsche's theory to say that it is unverifiable; nor again to say that, if you speak of a 'first creation' of ethical values, you must have in mind some datable event (whereas according to Nietzsche the same event takes place again and again, wherever the blond-haired 'Aryan' sets his conquering foot). The myth can even survive the largest objection of all: that there are no new starts in history, and that conquerors, like everyone else, must be burdened with a past and be inheritors of ancient traditions and constraints.

We shall certainly be eager to reject Nietzsche's myth because of its appalling fruits, but our grounds for rejecting it must be of a different kind. Its real weakness is that we can detect in it a bad faith on Nietzsche's part, of a kind basic to all his attitudes. He is—and no one could be better aware of it than himself—a nay-sayer who is masquerading as a yea-sayer. By nature Nietzsche is a masochist, inescapably convinced that he, personally, will always be on the wrong side. Possessing so great a genius, he has seen very deeply into the masochist plight, and there is no more acute diagnostician of the 'hoarse, groaning note of self-contempt', which he traces in most nineteenth-century literature and thought. Nevertheless, it is with the self-despisers that he himself belongs, as he once expressed in a heroic and unforgettable remark: 'What I am not, that for me is good and virtue.'

This said, something very valuable survives from Nietzsche's myth, of a conquering élite imposing its own natural characteristics as the moral law. Indeed, he seems to have put his finger on a central, though elusive, fact about 'the social'. It is this: that, by a very strong instinct, people are impelled to invoke aristocratic values even when, by so doing, they might seem to be putting themselves at a disadvantage or betraying their own cause. (It goes along with that other—not particularly attractive—trait in humans, that I have mentioned: that they cling to the luxury of stigmatizing some others as a 'rabble'.) Thus, to take an example, the peasants of Le Roy Ladurie's Montaillou use 'peasant' and 'rustic' as terms of insult. 'An inhabitant of the Pays d'Aillour who was dying insulted the priest who brought him the Eucharist by calling him a vile, stinking rustic.'[3]* Or again, we see John Lilburne, though he is a Leveller, defending the principle of private property in the most cavalier-like language imaginable:

For as for industry and *valour* by which the societies of mankind are maintained and preserved, who will take pains for that which when he has gotten is not his own, but must be equally shared in, by every lazy, simple, dronish sot? or who will fight for that, wherein he has no interest but such as must be subject to the will and pleasure of another, yea of every *coward and base lowspirited fellow*, that in his sitting still must share in common with a *valiant* man in all his *brave noble* achievements?[4]

It is a paradox which is always faintly scratching at one's mind, whatever period of history one happens to be studying. I note it again in the language used by Robert Owen to condemn the 'Manchester school' and the system of economic free-for-all.

It is a *low, vulgar, ignorant and inferior* mode of conducting the affairs of society; and no permanent, general and substantial improvement can arise until it shall be superseded by a superior mode of forming character and creating wealth.[5]

It is a positively ducal choice of language and undoubtedly sounds oddly on the lips of a pioneer Socialist.

The explanation, I suggest, is not to be looked for where Nietzsche locates it, in some unilateral imposition by a conquering élite, but in something more like a social contract. It has been perceived as an advantage by parties on both sides of the fence, the unprivileged as

---

* Cf. W. S. Holdsworth's remark concerning fourteenth-century Durham: 'On one of the Durham manors to call one another "rusticus" is made an offence—though in many cases the impeachment would undoubtedly have been true' (*History of English Law*, Book 2, 1909, p. 314).

well as the privileged, that the distinction between 'social' and 'ethical' should be blurred, and that when terms like 'noble', 'generous', 'base', 'vulgar' are used, it should be unclear whether it is a social or a moral judgement. We remember Proust's neat pinpointing of this mechanism in his Baron de Charlus, who could only appreciate beautiful women if they came of ancient family, and who would praise them by means of a sort of pun upon 'noble':

M. de Charlus would extol the true 'nobility' of spirit and heart of these women, thus playing upon the word with an equivocation which deceived even himself and in which resided the falsity of that bastard conception, that ambiguity between aristocracy, generosity and art, but also its seductiveness . . . [6]

The blurring, so far as one can see, has been pervasive and habitual in the past; and this fact itself is a warning not to posit some original 'conqueror-like' coup or confidence-trick. In the case of England, for instance, we would be very rash to blame it on the Norman Conquest, for in quite late medieval times it is still continually a problem whether someone or something is being praised or blamed for ethical qualities or merely for pertaining to the right or the wrong social 'set'. Equally it is striking how often ethical virtues and high social position are lumped together, as though logically inseparable. Medieval aldermen in London, when issuing summonses to their wardmotes, summoned the 'most sufficient', the 'most valiant' and the 'most powerful' citizens; and the valour and sufficiency (terms with an ethical colouring) were understood as the same things as wealth, or the ability to contribute to public charges—with the corollary that these, the more 'sufficient' citizens, were also the *better* people. 'These official phrases', says Sylvia Thrupp in *The Merchant Class of Medieval London* (1948) 'were not a mere empty traditional formula but represented a conscious blending of moral, economic, and political considerations.'[7] Before anyone could obtain the legal status of enfranchised citizen he had to prove his qualifications on all these three counts, and in recognition of this all citizens were by courtesy termed 'good folk' (*bons gens*). Likewise, when the poorer citizens and the unenfranchised were spoken of contemptuously, as a bad sort of people, it was with reference (implied or explicit) to their inability to pay taxes, their general ignorance, or their lack of experience in public affairs.

Evidently, what we are faced with here is not inability to distinguish ethics from social position, and we are not tracing the birth of ethics or 'genealogy of morals'. For after all, medieval Christendom can hardly be supposed ignorant of a certain 'pure' set of moral values, the specifically Christian ones. (Nor would Nietzsche recognize his blond-haired conquerors in these well-heeled medieval burgesses.) The blurring of ethics and social position here is not a relic but a conscious and purposive mechanism.

It has been a theme of this book that certain important social concepts, like 'bourgeois' and 'gentleman', are best thought of as rhetorics. They are devices that enable their users to swivel at will, and bewilderingly, between the social and the ethical (in the case of 'bourgeois' for purposes of vilification, in the case of 'gentleman' for purposes of recommendation). Perhaps the 'purposive mechanism' I am now discussing is, in a way, a paradigm of all such rhetorics.

It certainly seems to have a function in State-building, being one of those devices by which social antagonisms are tacitly adjusted and accommodated. We have already had an example in the business of the 'gentleman' in the seventeenth century. The logic of that is clear. When gentility is being discussed at the ideal level, enormous claims will be advanced for it. It will be made to seem an awe-inspiring condition, almost beyond human capacity; and it will be hedged round by a mystique, which will make all hope of joining the gentry seem almost vain. This mystique will employ Circularity and Deliberate Paradox. Circularity says: 'gentility' is the way in which gentlemen behave, so by definition it cannot be acquired by an outsider. Deliberate Paradox says: gentility is a matter of 'birth', 'blood', 'breeding', and 'family'. To this we object, and are *meant* to object: 'But everyone is born, everyone has blood, everyone has a family'; to which the reply, from across the fence, is: 'Yes, but not in our sense. Our position gives us the right to talk in mysteries.' It is quite another matter, however, at the practical level: that is to say, when people actually take steps to be called 'gentleman'. In such a case, by tacit agreement, the barriers are drastically lowered, and the process is made relatively easy and painless.

This is merely one example of a 'purposive mechanism' which in the past has been felt to be necessary to the running of a society. Yves Castan gives a very helpful analysis of another. He is describing how, when rustic citizens of eighteenth-century Languedoc got into a court of law, they would find themselves faced with a dilemma. In the language used by the judges and lawyers it would, on the one hand, be implied that *honnêteté* was a purely aristocratic perquisite (anyway it was a Parisian refinement that had hardly yet reached Languedoc). Yet on the other hand, and contradictorily, it would appear that it was expected of *them*, of rural shopkeepers and farmers. They apparently had a duty not just to be law-abiding, but to display *honnêteté*. Castan explains:

The fact of applying the term *honnête* to the well-off and leisured upper class is not a semantic restriction, it is an ambiguity found in all societies—i.e. the attributing to a society's élite, as though it were peculiar to them, a quality which in other contexts is declared to be the duty of everyone. It is in fact one of the most efficacious props of the social order, for it guarantees to the one set of people, on the grounds of their social position, the full enjoyment of that state of grace, and imposes on the rest a continual testing of their own merit. The legal use of such notions is particularly efficacious. No doubt the law clearly specifies misdemeanours and crimes and does not have to depend on that ethical criterion when imposing its judgements and penalties. But if it is not to become a pure nominalism—a crime being wholly defined by the letter of the law—the language of the law-court has continually to refer to generally accepted values and to seek the approval of the *honnêtes* by showing that one is only punishing the *malhonnêtes*.[8]

We may compare a remark by Walter Bagehot, in *The English Constitution* (1867): 'As long as we keep up a double set of institutions—one dignified and intended to impress the many, the other efficient and intended to govern the many—we should take care that the two match nicely, and hide where the one begins and the other ends.'[9]

J. G. Peristiany raises an issue rather similar to this in *Honour and Shame*. In his article 'Honour and Social Status' he argues that certain Mediterranean societies depend for their functioning on an ambiguity in the word 'honour' (or its local equivalent)—an equivocation between honour meaning virtuous and admirable behaviour and honour in the sense of 'honours' (as in 'Birthday Honours'). He speaks of those 'confusions' which centre on the conflicting meanings of the word 'honour': honour which derives from virtuous conduct and that honour which situates an individual socially and determines his right to precedence. 'The two senses', he says, 'appear to be so far removed from one another that one may ask why they were, and still are, expressed by the same word, why the languages of Europe are so determined to avoid clarity in this matter.' The explanation, he says, is that the confusion is in the interests of everybody.

Transactions of honour . . . serve these purposes: they not only provide, on the psychological side, a nexus between the ideals of society and their reproduction in the actions of individuals—honour commits men to act as they should (even if opinions differ as to how they should act)—but, on the social side, between the ideal order and the terrestrial order, validating the realities of power and making the sanctified order of precedence correspond to them. Thus, thanks to its duality, honour does something which the philosophers say they cannot do: derive an *ought* from an *is*; whatever *is* becomes *right*, the *de facto* is made *de jure*, the victor is crowned with laurels, the war-profiteer is knighted, the tyrant becomes the monarch, the bully, a chief. The reconciliation between the social order as we find it and the social order which we revere is accomplished thanks to the confusion which hinges upon the duality of honour and its associated concepts.[10]

My eye lights, though, on the word 'confusion'. For the word might be thought to suggest that the people involved do not know what they are doing, whereas I would suppose they know perfectly well. The logic of their behaviour is intricate but sound. The code of honour forbids a man to admit publicly that he is in the wrong, even if he is so and knows it and everyone else knows it too. This is a basic rule of 'honour' (and, for instance, underlies the duel). Now this rule has a justification in a higher rule and one which is, or may be, basic to the whole theory of the State, viz., that the king can do no wrong. That is to say, what the king does is right because it is he who does it; or to use Peristiany's words: 'What he [the king] *is* guarantees the evaluation of his actions.'[11] It is, accordingly, absolutely incumbent on citizens of 'honour and shame' societies to pay lip-service to the 'honours' that their monarch creates and bestows; for, however hollow these may be, they vindicate the honour-based mode of life. We need not imagine them as 'confused' in doing so.

Certainly in England (though of course it is not exactly the sort of society that Peristiany has in mind) the 'honours' transaction seems to have been instituted in a very open-eyed fashion. When the bestowing of honours was systematized, at the very end of the Middle Ages, it was done on the basis of ascribing powers or virtues that, palpably, the recipients did *not* possess. An earl was no longer a royal functionary, and an eminent City man who was knighted was not a warrior and had presumably never donned a helmet or wielded a lance in his life. Herein, precisely, lay the beauty of the compliment. Royal compliments are paid in the most highly prized currency.

In Hindu India, according to Louis Dumont in *Homo Hierarchicus* (1966), the currency of public esteem is not military value but purity. Thus the members of a caste, in a given locality, may acquire dominance in a quite familiar 'Western' way, i.e. by accumulating wealth or political influence, but their social superiority will be expressed in the currency of superior *purity*. 'We are not claiming that this fundamental distinction [the religious distinction between the pure and the impure] is the cause of all the caste-distinctions,' writes Dumont, 'we are claiming that it is their *form*.'[12] Something similar is true of landed property in Britain. Social historians have been known to write as though, in the seventeenth and eighteenth centuries in Britain, only the landed gentry 'counted' socially. This is patently absurd. But evidently why great lawyers, financiers, churchmen, or writers 'counted' (as they did) was not because they bought themselves some acres of the countryside, and played mine host to their tenants once a year, or served on the Commission of Peace. That was merely the token or the *form* of social success.

I have tried once or twice, earlier, to identify an area I have called 'the purely social', as preliminary to discovering how it fits into the political. The sort of mechanism I have been discussing in the present chapter perhaps suggests something about how it does so, or at least how it has done so in the past. What has tended to be required is some such equivocation, or 'bastard conception', as the Baron de Charlus's 'noble'. State-building demands at least nominal adhesion to a single social standard and requires, too, that the standard should (language aiding) appear to be the same as the ethical standard: that 'noble' meaning 'belonging to the nobility' should be the same word as 'noble' meaning 'of heroic and admirable character'. The process has had a parallel in public architecture. The State would attempt to make a spectacle of its virtue, adorning the monuments of its power with uplifting and 'improving' emblems, thereby suggesting an identity of power with virtue.

'A system of ruling-out'

All this is changed by the advent of 'class'. The concept of 'class' is rhetorical too, as we have seen, but in a different manner. (The equivocation in 'class' is not between the social and the ethical but between the evaluative and the value-free: it is a way of evaluating people, which yet offers itself as an objective fact or *fait accompli*.) The ethical plays no part in the theory of 'class', as it did so strongly in the case of 'rank', 'order', 'degree', etc. Likewise the State does not impose or endorse 'class', indeed it only rather reluctantly acknowledges its existence. But indeed, altogether, the State has progressively abnegated its 'improving' role, and no longer—in its buildings, or its law-courts, or its rituals—does it try to make a spectacle of its virtue.

'Class' thus seems to correspond to, and to represent, a tendency towards social dispersion and separation. As we saw, an 'honour'-based conception of society requires belief in an unclassified 'mob' or 'rabble', out of the circle of honour. 'Class'-theory, on the other hand, claims to classify everybody—the corollary of this being that, on the analogy of natural-history classification, the places it provides are based entirely on exclusion. A Species or Family in natural-history classification is, after all, not something positive, it is arrived at by exclusion and merely represents what is left when everything else has been excluded; and this exclusive character is carried over into 'class' as a social concept. There is nothing positive about being 'upper class'. It is not a fit object for pride and carries no rich, confused burden of connotation like being a 'lord' or 'gentleman'; it means purely and simply *not* being 'middle class', *not* being 'lower' (or 'working') class. 'Class' is essentially concerned with barriers.

When English people discuss 'class' it is significant that they feel on much firmer ground when talking about 'class-distinction' than about those elusive entities the 'classes', whose nature and boundaries seem so fluid. There is good reason for this, as was once pointed out by Evelyn Waugh. When in 1956 Nancy Mitford and Alan Ross reprinted their articles on 'U' and non-'U' in a volume *Noblesse Oblige*, they included an 'Open Letter' from Waugh, in which he quietly rebuked Nancy Mitford for being silly—for talking as if there were an immemorial and (below all appearances) unchanging 'upper class' in Britain. He made some extremely perceptive points in it (though, as one would expect with Waugh, with a smack of what I have called 'unholy pleasure', a perverse and coat-trailing advocacy of snobbery). He pretended to derive the terms 'upper, middle, and lower classes' from the professional habits of dons, acquired in grading undergraduate essays. Neither these terms, nor 'capitalists, bourgeois, intellectuals, workers', argued Waugh, apply in Britain, where there is very little 'horizontal stratification', apart from the 'single, variable, great divide' between 'gentleman and non-gentleman'. There is instead imaginary precedence:

a single wholly imaginary line (a Platonic idea) stretching from Windsor to Wormwood Scrubs, of separate individuals each justly and precisely graded. In the matter of talking together, eating together, sleeping together, this mysterious line makes little difference, but every Englishman is sharply aware of its existence, and this awareness often spices these associations very pleasantly.[13]

Again, on the negativity of modern social judgements, he wrote:

the basic principle of English social life is that *everyone* (everyone, that is to say, who comes to the front door) *thinks he is a gentleman*. There is a second principle of almost equal importance: *everyone draws the line of demarcation immediately below his own heels*. The professions rule out the trades; the Services, the professions; the Household Brigade, the line regiments; squires, squireens; landed families who have London houses rule out those who spend all the year at home; and so on, in an infinite number of degrees and in secret, the line is, or was, drawn. It is essentially a process of ruling *out*. If you examine the accumulated code of precepts which define 'the gentleman', you will find that almost all are negative.[14]

This, though faintly jarring in its tone, is actually very helpful; and it is as sceptical as one might wish towards the concepts of 'class' and of the 'gentleman'.

'Invisibility'

'Class' goes also, it would seem, with a desire for social invisibility. One should distinguish 'invisibility' from 'exclusivity'. No doubt the *honnête homme* would in his heart have preferred to spend all his time among his fellow *honnêtes gens*, and you could call this exclusivity; but as a man-of-the-world he could not expect it, and his social equipment was precisely designed for dealing with promiscuous company.

Equally one must distinguish 'invisibility' from 'distance', the preserving of a distance from one's superiors or inferiors—as when, in the time of Charles I, it was said of the Earl of Arundel by his secretary that 'He was a great master of order and ceremony, and knew and kept greater distance towards the sovereign than any person I ever observed, and expected no less from his inferiors.'[15] 'Distance' requires visibility, and can perhaps even be reduced to measurement (you are to keep distant by so many paces, etc.). It constitutes a positive relationship and carried no suggestion of hiding away, or going one's own way.

As Mark Girouard has pointed out,[16] it was a great step forward when, in the eighteenth century, the socially grand in England renounced the pleasures of 'distance' (or what Goldsmith called their 'Gothic haughtiness') and agreed to take part in 'general society'. The development is symbolized by the invention of the 'parade' and seems to have taken some of its impetus from Beau

Nash in Bath (the place where the term 'parade' seems first to have been used in an architectural sense). Girouard speaks of the development of 'polite society' or 'united society', where the great mixed with the humbler on equal terms, as a characteristic achievement of the eighteenth century; and it represents, clearly, one of those modifications of 'honour' I was speaking of earlier.

This giving up of the pleasures of 'distance', however, seems to develop in inverse proportion to something which is distinct from it and which seems unconnected with 'honour', viz., a desire for 'invisibility'. The classic anecdotes about 'invisibility' belong, significantly, to the heyday of the 'class' era. In Britain they tend to be associated with the great late Victorian and Edwardian country houses. Piers Brendon, in his history of the Guinness family, relates that at the Guinness mansion, Elveden, in Norfolk, servants were expected to be invisible to their employers at all times, and that the same was true of other great houses, like Woburn and Crewe Hall: 'If a member of the family or a guest appeared the servants were supposed to vanish, to dart down a passage, to hide in a cupboard or behind a hedge, or, failing that, simply to face the nearest wall'.[17]*

Such a passion for invisibility catches the imagination by its strangeness, and it does not seem to have any place in an honour-system. At first sight, indeed, it seems to relate to that tendency in seventeenth-century house-design which, by the provision of back stairs, closets and servants' rooms, made servants, in Mark Girouard's words, 'if not invisible, very much less visible'. I am inclined to think, though, that it should not be confused with this and that what was at work, rather, at Elveden, was the desire not to be seen *by* servants. It is not a matter of holding servants at a distance, which would carry with it a certain gratification (the enhancement of one's dignity). On the contrary, confrontation with servants for the employer at these country houses is purely embarrassing and painful.

We may explain it thus. It is not that the Edwardian grandee feels himself to be more great and god-like even than his ancestors. It is rather that in a democratic community there is no socially approved outlet for his sense of his own greatness. Thus the wish to assert it induces guilt-feelings; the pattern resembles that of neurosis.

---

* 'The gentry walking up the stairs no longer met their last night's faeces coming down them. Servants no longer bedded down in the drawing room, or outside their master's door or in a truckle bed at his feet. They became, if not invisible, very much less visible.' (*Life in the English Country House* (Penguin edn., 1980)) p. 138.

To what extent in Victorian Britain there came to be a reciprocal wish for invisibility, an effort of those in some superior/inferior relationship to be mutually invisible, is hard to decide. Victorian writers certainly asserted such a phenomenon. Robert Kerr writes in *The Gentleman's House* (1854):

It becomes the foremost of all maxims . . . that the Servants' Department shall be separable from the main house, so that what passes on either side of the boundary shall be both invisible and inaudible to the other . . . The idea which underlies all is simply this. The family constitutes one community: the servants another. Whatever may be to their mutual regard and confidence as dwellers under the same roof, each class is entitled to shut its door upon the other, and be alone . . . On both sides this privacy is highly valued.[18]

Again, the mid-Victorian census-reporter Horace Mann, attempting to explain the boycott of the churches by the working class, writes that 'the labouring myriads have no desire to mingle with persons of a higher grade'.[19] These are obviously tendentious statements, yet there may be something in them. One may surmise, for instance, that late nineteenth-century 'Cockney' speech-habits were a deliberate exaggeration and caricature on the part of East End Londoners, designed to exclude West Enders.

What seems to colour Victorian and Edwardian 'invisibility' and makes it so different from mere *honnête* reserve, is *embarrassment*—that sophisticated emotion which is so close to so-called 'primitive' feelings. I am impressed by Norbert Elias's book *The Civilising Process*,[20] which attributes great historical significance to embarrassment and embarrassments. It is Elias's theory that quite intimate psychological phenomena, like the advancing threshold of what people find physically embarrassing or indecent, express—under the sign of 'civilisation'—large politico-historical trends and events. He has a passage analysing a sequence of late medieval drawings, known as *The Medieval House-Book*, in which everyday life is depicted with an odd directness and lack of censorship: it shows lordly lovers, and an old servant pulling an angry face at their love-games; a ragged peasant disembowelling a dead horse, and a pig sniffing at his posterior; labourers quarrelling; beggars with outstretched hands; a gallows. It is a 'knightly' vision, but very different from later aristocratic art, which needs to emphasize and exclude. Elias comments: 'There is no identification of man with man. Not even on the horizon of this life is there an idea that all men are "equal". But perhaps for that very reason the sight of the labourers has about it nothing shameful or embarrassing.'[21]

This is a familiar enough perception about medieval art, and similar things are said sometimes about Chaucer. However, it is sharpened by Elias's stress on 'embarrassment' and by his equation of unembarrassment with the lack of identification of man with man. What we find in the 'honour'-systems that I have discussed is, of course, not exactly lack of identification of man with man, but most certainly a consciously *limited* identification of man with man. ('General benevolence or charity are not demanded of people. You may leave a dying man unaided, having ascertained that he has no claim on you by reason of kinship, neighbourliness, or related interests.')[22] It brings home to us how much the intense embarrassment of master and men in Edwardian Elveden or Woburn has sprung from fuller self-identification of man with man—what Lévi-Strauss has called 'that perfidious dose of homogeneity . . . which permits comparison';*—an obligation impossible to escape in the centuries after Rousseau.

This suggests something about the genesis of 'class' as a concept. It can be seen as hinging upon the *unlimited*. It is intrinsic to a social 'class' that, unlike an 'order', it is unlimited, imposing no ceremony of admission. (The first of the 'leading rules' of the London Corresponding Society was: 'That the number of our Members be unlimited.') Equally, in its pure negativity it represents a *resistance* to an unlimited demand, viz., that we should identify with every other member of the community or the human race. This is a demand which grows more and more imperious in the nineteenth century. The corollary to George Eliot's scorn for the Dodson and Clegg outlook is her insistence that we should be continually widening the range of our sympathies, nor be contented till we embrace the whole of humanity. To this demand 'class' offers an assent, but a chilly one. A 'class', by nature, will be no sheltering and humanly uniting institution. 'Class' is ready to find a place for everybody, both living and yet to be born, but only on condition that no further bond is expected beyond mere position.

* 'It is tragic for mankind that that great experiment [the Hindu caste-system] has failed, I mean that over the course of history castes have not succeeded in achieving a situation where they would remain equal because different—equal in the sense that they were incommensurable—and that perfidious dose of homogeneity has been introduced among them which permits comparison, and hence the creation of a hierarchy' (C. Lévi-Strauss, *Tristes tropiques*, 1955, p. 128).

It follows that a Marxist-style campaign for 'class-solidarity' will have the force of a paradox. It will imply the overcoming of what is most natural to members of 'classes', atomization. The point is echoed by Sartre when he argues that we only achieve solidarity, we can only acquire a sense of being 'us', through oppression—through becoming the victim of an indifferent gaze for which we are so many objects or instruments.[23] It is not possible to take pleasure in being a member of a 'class'. This does not mean that, when it comes to 'class-*solidarity*', very honourable and indeed heroic feelings may not be involved: it was so, for instance, at the birth of the 'working class'. There must always be a proviso, though—something on the lines of, 'If there *have* to be classes, I intend to be loyal to mine.' It does not seem humanly possible to love one's 'class' wholeheartedly, though one may love one's fellows in it, since at the root of 'classes' and 'class-solidarity' there lies an evil necessity. Sartre is surely right when he says that thinking oneself as part of an 'Us' corresponds to an experience of humiliation and impotence?[24] The memory stirs in our mind of that petrifying stare by which the Other (that is to say here another 'class') turns one into a mere object, and in so doing constitutes us as a 'class'. (Sartre speaks of it as the 'deep meaning' of the myth of the Medusa.)

In Lawrence's *Sons and Lovers* there is a very attractive passage in which Paul argues with his mother about his 'class' position.

'You know,' [Paul] said to his mother, 'I don't want to belong to the well-to-do middle class. I like my common people best. I belong to the common people.'

'But if anybody else said so, my son, wouldn't you be in a tear. You know you consider yourself equal to any gentleman.'

'In myself,' he answered, 'not in my class or my education or my manners. But in myself I am.'

'Very well, then. Then why talk about the common people?'

'Because—the difference between people isn't in their class, but in themselves. Only from the middle classes one gets ideas, and from the common people—life itself, warmth. You feel their hates and loves.'

'It's all very well, my boy. But, then, why don't you go and talk to your father's pals?'

'But they're rather different.'

'Not at all. They're the common people. After all, whom do you mix with now—among the common people? Those that exchange ideas, like the middle class. The rest don't interest you.'[25]

Lawrence is expecting us to do a lot of 'unpacking' here. The point is that, perfectly rightly, Paul wants it all ways. He wants the feeling of not being disloyal to his own 'class'; he also definitely wants a life, not only of 'warmth' but of ideas; and he renders this consistent by engineering his mother's part of the argument, forcing *her* to make the relevant objections. The concepts ('from the middle classes one gets ideas' etc.) are naïve, but the fictional thought is far from naïve and indeed most subtle; though a legitimate gloss on it would be that Paul is really railing against the whole idea of 'classes'.

The passage contrasts with a dispirited one in a late 'Autobio-graphical Sketch', in which Lawrence comes back to something like Paul's typology of the 'classes', but to very different effect.

Then why don't I live with my working people? Because their vibration is limited in another direction. They are narrow, but still fairly deep and pas-sionate, whereas the middle class is broad and shallow and passionless. Quite passionless. At the best they substitute affection, which is the great middle-class positive emotion.

But the working class is narrow in outlook, in prejudice, and narrow in intelligence. This again makes a prison. One can belong absolutely to no class.[26]

Here the 'unpacking' we do has to be at Lawrence's expense, for the next two paragraphs give the game away. Though he 'can belong absolutely to no class', he takes pleasure, he says, in 'a certain silent contact' with the peasants who work the land round his villa (he is living in Italy). He is not intimate with them, he hardly speaks to them except to say good day, nor are they working for him. 'Yet it is they, really, who form my *ambiente*, and it is from them that the human flow comes to me.' The rationalization strikes one as forlorn, for what he really wants to say, we feel, is simply that 'contact' no longer interests him.

As for the larger question, whether the whole way of thought called 'class' is a good thing, it is hard to think of legitimate reasons for considering it so, though one can think of some 'unholy' ones. Those who say to themselves that the concept of 'class' is a useful intellectual tool, which they can use whilst standing outside the 'class-system', seem just to be deluding themselves, in a not very reputable way; indeed this is the root of much that is most mis-chievous in the concept of 'class'. More acceptable is the attitude of those who resign themselves to 'class' as something that is *there* and will not go away, and who say to themselves 'I don't much enjoy being classed, but I suppose I cannot complain, since I am doing it all the time to others.'

For a swingeing statement of the case against 'class' I may quote the concluding words of Peter Calvert's book *The Concept of Class* (1982).

Should we, therefore, abandon the concept of class altogether? The answer is almost certainly yes. As a legal concept, it has had its day. As an economic concept, it has too many snags to be measured. As an evaluation of social status, the use of the word serves only to blur the evaluative use of the word 'status' itself. This, being itself of respectable ancestry, could well serve to represent this curious quirk of the human mind for as long as human beings continue to practise such evaluations.

Whether or not they should be encouraged to make such evaluations about one another and to state them as fact is another matter. Our present century has already seen the elimination of a number of forms of discrimination between religions, between races and between the sexes. Racism is widely regarded as abhorrent. Religious bigotry is undergoing something of a revival but there are hopeful signs that this revival is far from universally welcomed. Sexism has hardly been touched upon except in the world's most liberal societies, just those, in fact, from which comes the majority of complaints about its persistence. But it is probably not too soon to consider tackling 'classism' on the same condition: that we work to eliminate arbitrary distinctions wherever they occur and regardless of the strength of those who give them currency.[27]

What one has to say about this, of course, is that, precisely, it comes at the very end of his book. One may agree with him that it would be good to put an end to 'class'-thinking, and he has suggested some powerful reasons. Still, he has not given us any clear proposal as to how we might go about it. Does the project make sense at all? And has anyone ever suggested a scheme by which we might escape from 'class'-thinking? Well, it occurs to me that, in a certain indirect way, they have; and this will form the subject of my final chapter.

10
*
The escape

There is no doubt that hearing too much talk about 'class', and all the more writing a book about it, gives one a longing for escape. It is an uneasy, enervating, somehow murky topic—a fact which no amount of bravado or 'scientism' can alter. Peter Calvert's view that 'class' is something akin to 'racism' and 'sexism' and that, like them, it may soon become taboo, is really very attractive, and one could construct an argument why the present might be the historical moment for this. The argument has to do with domestic service, or rather with the abolition of domestic service in Britain round about 1939.

I am inclined to regard the period from the 1830s to the 1930s as constituting, from the point of view of the 'purely social', a unity. In all sorts of ways we found its beginning a very important date for our subject. This was the time of the first Reform Act, thus symbolically the opening of the egalitarian era; it was the moment at which 'class' terminology took its rise in Britain; and it was a decade, so at least it appeared to many commentators, when a mania for 'gentility' and for social striving raged through the land. Hardly less important for us, though, I am inclined to suggest, was the end-date of the period, which I have for convenience fixed at 1939—this being the moment when it ceased to be expected in Britain that householders should employ living-in servants.

I am not writing a social history of Britain, but let me just sketch one tableau, which shall be dated vaguely in the 1860s or later. By this time a person regarding himself as a 'gentleman' is no longer part of an 'outward-honour' system; and appropriately he will be wearing a drab costume, aiming neither at 'fineness' nor at beauty; it is a 'modest' costume, a belated legacy of that swerve towards modesty which we observed in the concept of the 'gentleman'. This gentlemanly householder of the 1860s will, however, have domestic servants, and these servants—as would not have been the case in the eighteenth century—are wearing a uniform. The maids will be in a recently invented uniform of cap, streamers, and apron. The footman if there is one, will be in the peacock-like garb of an eighteenth-century fine gentleman; his costume, by remaining unchanged over the years, whilst his employer has changed to drab suit and chimney-pot hat, has become a 'uniform', and a peculiarly freakish-looking one. Even the butler will be distinguished by some deliberate sartorial solecism—the 'wrong' tie or trousers. Thus there is no difficulty in knowing servant from employer—a matter of importance because of a new rule, that a 'gentleman' may not assert his own gentility and must merely hope to have it acknowledged. 'Gentility' is by now always contestable and a matter of doubt; and accordingly non-gentility has to be signalled *beyond* all doubt.

What these sartorial changes are meant to proclaim, too, is that the old 'service-based' society is finally dead. It was once no indignity to be 'in service'. How else should even a high-born young man rise than by being in the service, and maybe in the livery, of some grandee? (One perceives that the concept of the 'snob' pertains to a later and egalitarian age; no one would pass a judgement of 'snobbery' on Pepys for his sedulous attentiveness to his 'Lord'.) Now, however, in the egalitarian age of the 1860s (the 'Services' and the Civil Service notwithstanding) dignity is equated with independence. It follows that to be a 'servant' will henceforth, automatically, spell social inferiority. In the contract of a domestic servant, his or her inferiority will be a tacit but essential clause (which indeed may be why some people will wish to acquire servants), and it will be totally acceptable socially to think or speak of servants as 'inferiors'. Thus at the 'purely social' level, as opposed to the political one, social divisions have actually been sharpened, or at least made more nakedly visible. The new attitude to 'service' presents a parallel to the concept of 'class', which, as we have seen, highlights superiority/inferiority more nakedly than earlier schemes.

Let us turn now to the post-1939 social scene. Servants, or at any rate the servant-system as arranged by the Victorians, have disappeared, and this fact has a surprisingly wide significance. Its effect has been, really, to make it no longer socially permissible to categorize a fellow-human as an inferior—certainly to speak of him or her as being so. It is a fact we are very much aware of in contemporary Britain, and not just because we have been told it, but from introspection and as a matter of intimate conviction. I am not speaking here of *feeling*; for who can say what individual Victorians, or individual members of the post-1939 era, felt or feel on the 'inferiority' issue? I am speaking rather of social law and concept. Quite quickly after 1939 a new rule was quietly added to 'decent' behaviour: viz., that a decent person considered no one as a social inferior.

Now this rule has large consequences for the concept of 'class'. 'Class' categorizes people as socially 'higher' and 'lower'. Thus henceforth as a concept it will have something disreputable about it, a maggot at its very core; it entails the assuming or making of a kind of valuing judgement which is actually under a ban. There is a kind of bad conscience or bad faith attaching to it, which will help explain the brassy tone in which henceforth it tends to be used.

So ours, then, is the time to escape from the concept of 'class', if there were a way of doing so? Or, on the other hand, is it too late to escape, and is that precisely what gives 'class' an evil and anachronistic hold over our minds, like a paler version of anti-Semitism?

My answer is that a mental escape-route from 'class' has already been proposed to us and has been on offer for some appreciable period of the past. It is the one indicated by certain novelists, especially some 'modernist' novelists—and in proportion to the degree of their 'modernism'—and before them by Dickens.

Lionel Trilling, in an essay of 1947 'Manners, Morals, and the Novel', argued that 'class' was the proper and destined subject-matter of the novel.[1] In fact, as I have already suggested (see p. 101) the great Victorian novelists made very little of 'class', in the strict sense. There is no need to be pedantic, however. 'Gentleman', as a concept, is by today more or less obsolete,* and 'rank', 'orders', 'degree' have been under a ban for a century or more. Thus the term 'class' has been left in possession of the field, as the omnibus name for social distinctions, social pretensions, social-shibboleth-making and so on; and we can agree that the novel has, in a sense, thriven on these topics.

In the same essay, Trilling writes that the appointed subject of the novel is not just manners in general, but manners from the point of view of snobbery. 'The characteristic work of the novel', he writes, 'is to record the illusion that snobbery generates and to try to penetrate to the truth which, as the novel assumes, lies hidden beneath all the false appearances.'[2] Again, as will have been seen (see pp. 17–18), I prefer the historical approach to the concept of 'snob-

---

* I like a remark by Robin Gilmour, in *The Idea of the Gentleman in the Victorian Novel*, (p.14) that 'something has gone seriously wrong' when Sir Edward Elgar can record his relief, at the Wembley Exhibition of 1924, at discovering a bunch of 'gentlemanly' daisies in the turf: 'Damn everything except the daisy—I was back in something sane, wholesome and *gentlemanly*.'

bery', and to regard it not as a 'timeless' concept but as one mainly relevant to an 'egalitarian' age. Still, we may allow Trilling his point. He wants to rebut the charge that the English novel, with its obsession with social *minutiae*, is trivial and shallow and fails 'to explore the deeper layers of personality'. 'Who cares?' he quotes an unnamed critic as expostulating:

Who cares whether Pamela finally exasperates Mr B. into marriage, whether Mr Elton is more or less than moderately genteel, whether it is sinful for Pendennis nearly to kiss the porter's daughter, whether young men from Boston can ever be as truly refined as middle-aged women in Paris, whether the District Officer's fiancée ought to be seeing so much of Dr Aziz, whether Lady Chatterley ought to be made love to by the gamekeeper, even if he was an officer during the war? Who cares?[3]

To this, Trilling's answer is that, if the English novel fails, it is not because of its 'class' preoccupations, for it shares these with novels to which everyone would grant profundity.

the French novel in exploring these deeper layers must start and end in class, and the Russian novel, exploring the ultimate possibilities of spirit, does the same—every situation in Dostoevski, no matter how spiritual, starts with a point of social pride and a certain number of rubles. The great novelists know that manners indicate the largest intentions of men's souls as well as the smallest and they are perpetually concerned to catch the meaning of every dim implicit hint.[4]

It is not a bad answer. And there is no question but that, as readers, we *do* care whether Mr Elton is genteel or not, and how little or much; Jane Austen manages to make it a matter of profound interest. All the same, and allowing some force in Trilling's thesis, I feel like saying that the more important truth is almost the opposite: I mean, that the true destiny of fiction, whatever is true of its origins, lay in transcending these 'class' preoccupations.

One cannot deny the fact, there are some things about the classic English novels which are wearisome. Their authors seem often to be playing some game, of great if tortuous ingenuity, yet somehow insulting to the reader. (We know what Virginia Woolf meant when she called *Middlemarch* one of the very few Victorian novels that seem to be written for adults.) When Meredith goes off into phantasmagoria, when Thackeray grows too avuncular, we know that they are dodging: they are reserving some part of their mind from us, as if we were not fit to be entrusted with it. The fact creates a sense of waste. Both Thackeray and Meredith were men of amazing talent, yet if one excepts *Vanity Fair*, it is hard not to think of their careers as in a certain sense *manqués*; one cannot feel towards them quite as one does towards Flaubert and Dostoevsky.

Now, one way of explaining, or anyway of describing, their failure is to say that they attribute too much authority to social 'absolutes'. I have already suggested a gloss on 'the gentleman' in the Victorian novel, viz., that the realistic, as opposed to the 'romance', message is a negative one and something to do with *non*-gentlemen—i.e. it is to encourage readers in the faith that they themselves must be gentlemen (or ladies) because they are able to pass the judgement that certain people are not gentlemen or ladies. However this may be, the important point is, the novels of Thackeray and Meredith and Trollope frequently take their very *form* from this 'absolute'. *Evan Harrington* is, in its structure, a suspense-story about gentility. It shows how, through many testings, Evan manages ultimately to prove himself a 'gentleman', whilst—this is the zest of the comedy—his sister the Countess, for all her Napoleonic social strivings, is never even for a moment on the track of being a 'lady'.

The 'gentlemanliness' at stake in *Evan Harrington* is of the 'manly' school, and a subsidiary theme, pursued with much subtlety, concerns 'manhood'. Evan's father, 'the great Mel', was a tailor, though in his leisure-hours he played the Regency buck; and a tailor is proverbially only one-ninth of a man. Where, then, shall Evan's 'manhood' lie: in following the instinct which tells him he is a 'gentleman' or in having the courage to face his 'Tailordom'? It is a brilliant and cunning design, indeed I am fond of the novel, yet one senses something faked and feverish in it. The tone proclaims an Olympian Meredith, detached and amused, concerned with 'gentlemanliness' and 'Tailordom' merely as food for comedy; but the message we actually receive is that Meredith is distinctly involved and anxious about these matters. On the crucial matter of Evan's 'gentlemanliness' he is ready to question and defy conventional opinion, but as a *quid pro quo* he must allow conventional opinion on the Countess—that she is not, and never could be, a 'lady'—to be without redress. The looks exchanged behind her back at Beckley Court are presented as definitive.

It will be clear that I am not passing a social judgement on Meredith, but an artistic one. The issue is partly about artistic opportunism. The truth is that social 'absolutes' are dangerously convenient to a novelist (somewhat as, at a simpler level, conventional sexual 'absolutes' have in the past proved convenient to the farce-writer).

They provide the novelist with a ready-made framework, which seems to him or her a great boon. There is, however, a price to be paid for this. It is always dangerous to the art of fiction when a novelist begins to behave as a *social* creature.

Thackeray provides important examples of this rule. His complicated relationship to his reader is to a marked extent a *social* relationship, exhibiting all the ruses of his socially hyperconscious personality. Observe the ingenious way in which, in *The Newcomes*, he resolves an equation about 'gentlemanliness'. He is so determined that Colonel Newcome shall be a perfect gentleman that it becomes a difficulty when a 'ruling-out' judgement has to be passed—for it adds another ray to the halo of a gentleman that he should be deeply loath to say someone else is *not* a gentleman or lady. Thackeray's solution, therefore, is to have the Colonel's schoolboy son voice the judgement.

'Uncle Hobson don't live in such good society as Uncle Newcome. You see, Aunt Hobson, she's very kind, you know, and all that, but I don't think she's what you call *comme il faut*.'

'Why, how are you to judge?' asked the father, amused at the lad's candid prattle, 'and where does the difference lie?'

'I can't tell you what it is, or how it is,' the boy answered, 'only one can't help seeing the difference. It isn't rank and that; only somehow there are some men gentlemen and some not, and some women ladies and some not. There's Jones now, the fifth-form master, every man sees he's a gentleman, though he wears ever so old clothes; and there's Mr. Brown, who oils his hair, and wears rings, and white chokers—my eyes! such white chokers!— and yet we call him the handsome snob! And so about Aunt Maria, she's very handsome and she's very finely dressed, only somehow she's not—she's not the ticket, you see.'[5]

That 'amused at the lad's candid prattle' is, in its deviousness, quintessentially Thackerayan; but there is, it seems to me, a touch of artistic bad faith in it.

The limitations of Trollope have their roots in the same problem. In *Can You Forgive Her?* (1864) he provides two tableaux, deliberately contrasted: Mrs Greenow's seaside picnic at Yarmouth, and the Edgehill meet. The hunting field, with its endlessly intricate coding, was a most important scene for Trollope, very fit to stand for England. It was more significant than a mere game, like cricket, since the social ties and conflicts involved stood close to reality. In its organization the hunt expressed his dearest wish, that the 'purely social' should predominate over or dictate to, the political: thus the master of the hunt has an absolute authority, entitling him to be as gruff and offensive as he pleases, in virtue of the fact that his authority is merely concessionary, not backed by power. Likewise the actual events of the chase offer a wide variety of testings of character and 'gentlemanliness' and of the gradations of the gentlemanly—the ultimate criterion being responsibility for the voteless and long-suffering horse. ('There are men who never know how little a horse can do,—or how much!'[6])

Chapter 17, 'Edgehill', in *Can You Forgive Her*? is an admirable piece of writing and makes it not absurd that Tolstoy should have expressed envy of Trollope. It makes a striking contrast with the tiresome seaside-picnic chapters in the same novel, with their satire on purse-proud farmers, bogus army-captains, and fading seaside charmers. Trollope is clumsy and faintly offensive in these pages, and the reason is a fundamental one: he does not believe that, in its very nature, a seaside picnic can be anything but vulgar or can connect with any serious human values. What is involved here is a social 'absolute', and temporarily it cripples him as an artist.

A more ambiguous example is provided by George Eliot in *Felix Holt*. In this novel, so much dominated by the concept of 'the gentleman', we sense that there is a social archetype or stereotype behind George Eliot's portrayal of Felix himself, viz., that he is a natural gentleman, or, as the phrase goes, 'one of Nature's Gentlemen'. We sense, too, that she is embarrassed by the fact; and to her credit she never, in fact, voices this concept in so many words. Still, it dimly makes its presence felt. At any rate this is a gloss that I would put on the fact, on which readers tend to agree, that Felix does not altogether come off as a character.

Let us consider, again, the curious case of Surtees. He is an extraordinarily gifted writer, and in reading *Mr Sponge's Sporting Tour* one is sometimes tempted to call him the English Gogol. Joyce Cary once wrote of him, very truly, that 'He has no cant of any kind; he is sucking up to nobody and no class';[7] and by reason of his cussed and sardonic truth-telling he is always taking one by surprise.

The moral schemes in his books are really very odd. In his first success, *Jorrocks' Jaunts and Jollities*, it is Jorrocks the Cockney grocer who has the princely virtues: though unashamedly vulgar, he is a hearty, if shrewd, spender and is made sublime by his passion for fox-hunting. By contrast his crony 'the Yorkshireman', a penniless man-about-town—representing the young Surtees himself—is an avowed sponger. The rules of their friendship are made explicit between them:

Now to business—Mrs J. is away at Tooting, as you perhaps knows, and I'm alone in Great Coram Street, with the key of the cellar, larder, and all that sort of thing, and I've a werry great mind to be off on a jaunt—what say? 'Not the slightest objection', replied the Yorkshireman, 'on the old principle of you finding cash, and me finding company.'[8]

Surtees, Thackeray, and Dickens are interlinked, in that all-important moment for the novel, the 1830s. Thackeray's reaction against the 'silver-fork' school of fiction is paralleled by Surtees's reaction against Apperley, its genteel sporting equivalent: and it was *Jorrocks* and its success which inspired *The Pickwick Papers*. Indeed there are passages in *Jorrocks* so funny and evocative, in a Dickensian way, that there must have been some direct influence on Dickens.*

For all this, the book does not take off, as one feels it might have done. The conception is stifled, not by cant, certainly, but by cliché. Implausibly, Jorrocks and his fellow-sportsmen are made to talk 'Exchange' business on the hunting-field, and the stalest and hoariest of genteel *idées reçues*—that 'commercial' types cannot follow classical allusions[9]—is laboriously staged. For much of the time, indeed, the book drops into thoroughly stupid farce: Jorrocks in Paris, making comic language-mistakes, is lamentable. Surtees's strange genius seems to me to have been hampered more than most by what I have termed social 'absolutes', as a temptation to artistic laziness.

The contrast with Dickens is striking. *Pickwick Papers* had a great strangeness for readers at the time. They could not believe their ears, or their luck, at this new thing that was offered to them: and the strangeness relates, I would suggest, to Dickens's rejection of social 'absolutes'. Let us take Mr Pickwick, for instance. He is, apparently, a retired 'City' man; and the stock reactions to this would be (old-style) that he is a vulgarian, or (new-style) that he is, or was, a sinister and exploitative *entrepreneur*. The innocence of Pickwick is, evidently, some kind of deliberate flouting of stock responses on Dickens's part. But, in fact, no purely social joke or judgement is made about Pickwick at all, nor do his origins have any bearing on the action which is entirely concerned with present—with the extraordinary phenomena he encounters when he sets out to inspect Eng-

---

* For instance the lovely scene of the early-morning meeting of Jorrocks and the Yorkshireman in the Piazza at Covent Garden.

land. It is in a similar way that, when the Pickwickians go to visit
Mr Wardle in the country, all 'feudal' references are suppressed:
there is no 'great house', or lord of the manor, overshadowing
Dingley Dell. If Wardle's farmhouse, and the village, are 'old-
English', they are so in a purposely quite ahistorical way.

The past, for Dickens, is essentially an old curiosity shop, a random
assemblage of miscellaneous objects most of which have lost their use, if
ever they had any; and among this debris are 'the gentleman' and
'gentlemanliness'. G. K. Chesterton's remark seems admirably just:

> When people say that Dickens could not describe a gentleman, what they
> mean is this, and so far what they mean is true. They mean that Dickens
> could not describe a gentleman as gentlemen feel a gentleman . . . when we
> talk of describing a gentleman, we always mean describing a gentleman
> from the point of view of one who either belongs to, or is interested in per-
> petuating, that type. Dickens did not describe gentlemen in the way that
> gentlemen describe gentlemen. He described them in the way in which he
> described waiters, or railway guards, or men drawing with chalk on the
> pavement. He described them, in short . . . from the outside, as he de-
> scribed any other oddity or special trade.[10]

Another way of putting Chesterton's point is to say that, unlike
Thackeray and Meredith, Dickens does not feel the compulsion to
enter into social relations with his characters, or to pass social judgement on them. He is in fact, in his own way, a very great expert on
gentility, niceties of honour, 'ruling-out' and all the rest of it, for they
are sure to raise their head in almost any social gathering that he is
depicting—in the shrimp and watercress tea-parties at Mrs Quilp's
lodgings on Tower Hill as at pompous dinners at Chesney Wold.
And the most beautiful joke in it, for him, is that the codes and
creeds and standards involved are much the same in whatever *milieu*.
Those wonderful evening parties at the Kenwigses in *Nicholas
Nickleby*, at which Mr Lillyvick the water-rate collector plays the
part of the great man, demanding and receiving the homage due to
such a character and shaking his will whenever it is not received, are
perfect exemplars of the whole system.* It is the real thing, whatever

---

* Thackeray, in an anonymous article , 'Horae Catnachianae', in *Fraser's Magazine*
(April 1839), imagines an Australian critic two thousand years hence scorning the
absurd theory that the English text of the works of 'Boz' was the original, when it was
plainly a totally inept translation, by somebody with no social knowledge, from the
German of the learned Lambert Bos, author of the *Greek Ellipses*. 'Lillyvick, a gentleman
of wealth and character—*steuereinnehmer*, tax-gatherer in the aristocratic realm of England—a humorist it is true (the wealthy often are so)—is made, by the English *traducer* (as
we call him), a low buffoon, of coarse habits, ignorant of the very principles of grammar.'

that reality means, when Mr Lillyvick receives Nicholas Nickleby
frostily:

'How do you do, sir?' said Mr Lillyvick—rather sharply; for he had not
known what Nicholas was, on the previous night, and it was rather an
aggravating circumstance if a tax collector had been too polite to a
teacher.[11]

Equally it is the real thing when Mrs Jarley of the Waxwork, in *The
Old Curiosity Shop*, expresses the utmost indignation at Nell's enquiry
whether she knows Codlin and Short, the Punch-and-Judy men:

'Know 'em, child!' cried the lady of the caravan in a sort of shriek. 'Know
them! But you're young and inexperienced, and that's your excuse for asking
sich a question. Do I look as if I know'd 'em, does the caravan look as if *it*
know'd 'em?'[12]

Nor is it any less the genuine social article, when Mrs Jarley, receiving the message from Miss Monflathers that she should be put in the
stocks for sending handbills to Miss Monflathers's school, goes
through all the phases of social shock: wrath, impotent vengefulness,
a solemn and despairing potation among her satellites, and finally
the magnanimity of helpless laughter.

   We are not to think of these scenes as a parody of high life (though
Dickens was also a great master of social parody), for part of the
glory of the joke, for him, is that the social standard to which his
characters are tacitly appealing does not actually exist, and would
be very inimical to happiness if it did. There is a connection here
with his dislike of Georgian architecture, with its frowning and
supercilious regularity—whether in the grand squares of Mayfair or
in miniature and mass-produced replica in the suburbs of his own
day. His own preference in architecture was for the wild variousness
of the neo-Gothic: and the social message of his novels is similar—
knock away the social standard, and there will be revealed to you all
the wild and marvellous variousness of England. Dickens's note is
not really a levelling one. He is concerned not to attack social distinctions and distinction-making as an Apollyon bestriding the way
but rather to wave these things aside as, ultimately, an irrelevance
and absurdity.

   He has, you might say, grasped the great principle of relativity.
Each social confrontation implies a definite vision of the 'social
order', but these visions do not, and could not possibly, agree—so
that it would be a vain task to try to extract from them a single com-

posite picture of the 'social order'. Many commentators, especially of the 1830s, fumbled at this conclusion, but their tone——lamenting, or censorious, or supercilious——shows they are not happy with it and are still hankering after social absolutes. We feel this with Lytton when he writes, in *England and the English*:

> These mystic, shifting, and various shades of graduation; these shot silk colours of society produce this effect: that people have no exact and fixed position——that by acquaintance alone they may rise to look down on their superiors——that while the rank gained by intellect, or by interest, is open but to few, the rank that may be obtained by fashion seems delusively to be open to all.[13]

It is Dickens's delight in this truth that guarantees his full acceptance of it; and it was from the start one of the greatest resources of his comedy. We remember the ball at Rochester in chapter 2 of *Pickwick*, at which the 'Dock-yard' and the 'Garrison' form rival aristocracies and offer themselves as model to 'the other classes of society'.

> 'Wait a minute,' said the stranger [Jingle], 'fun presently——nobs not come yet——queer place——Dock-yard people of upper rank don't know Dock-yard people of lower rank——Dock-yard people of lower rank don't know small gentry——small gentry don't know tradespeople——Commissioner don't know anybody.'
>
> 'Who's that little boy with the light hair and pink eyes, in fancy dress?' inquired Mr Tupman.
>
> 'Hush, pray——pink eyes——fancy dress——little boy——nonsense——Ensign 97th——Honourable Wilmot Snipe——great family——Snipes——very.'
>
> 'Sir Thomas Clubber, Lady Clubber, and the Miss Clubbers!' shouted the man at the door in a stentorian voice. A great sensation was created throughout the room by the entrance of a tall gentleman in a blue coat and bright buttons, a large lady in blue satin, and two young ladies, on a similar scale, in fashionably made dresses of the same hue.
>
> 'Commissioner——head of the yard——great man——remarkably great man,' whispered the stranger in Mr Tupman's ear . . . While the aristocracy of the place——the Bulders, and Clubbers, and Snipes——were thus preserving their dignity at the upper end of the room, the other classes of society were imitating their example in other parts of it. The less aristocratic officers of the 97th devoted themselves to the families of the less important functionaries from the Dock-yard. The solicitors' wives, and the wine-merchant's wife, headed another grade (the brewer's wife visited the Bulders); and Mrs Tomlinson, the post-office keeper, seemed by mutual consent to have been chosen the leader of the trade party.

Who is to decide the relative status of 'Dock-yard' and 'Garrison'?

There is no written code or authority to which this question can be referred, no ideal scale in which 'Dock-yard' and 'Garrison' have their appointed rank; and this, of course, is precisely what Dickens is conveying.

If relativity is a great principle for Dickens, it may be said that it became, after him, a leading concern for serious novelists in general, and more especially for *avant-garde* ones. It began almost to appear, you might say, as the great discovery that fiction had to offer. Continually to be playing off one human consciousness against another, to be confronting one private image of the world with another utterly different one, thereby unsettling stock ideas of reality—this, more and more, seemed to 'modernizing' novelists their appointed occupation. The truths towards which novelists strive (and of course they do strive after truths) are attained only after prolonged immersion in relativity; and in this immersion many imaginary 'absolutes' are of necessity dissolved, among them social ones like 'the gentleman', 'class' etc. A broad 'modernist' doctrine, common to poets and to novelists, also comes in here, viz., that, so far as possible, all pre-existing categories, classifications and 'frames' should be dispensed with, in the cause of 'unmediated vision' and direct commerce with 'the thing itself'. Thus it would have been against the 'modernist' spirit for a novelist to establish social relations with his characters and to act as, as it were, the social intermediary between them and the reader.

The new philosophy of fiction necessarily brought with it technical change. It had to lead, in the first place, to innovation in prose style; for the cadences and contentions of 'educated' prose evidently carry a very strong charge of social assumptions. (One thinks of Forster, who plays so brilliantly on the inflexions of 'educated' speech and achieves much subversiveness by means of it, yet remains to some degree a prisoner—a conscious prisoner—of social absolutes.)

It would lead, also, to the taking of certain quite basic disciplinary vows. I am thinking, for instance, of Proust, who adopted a technical principle which is an expression of 'relativism' at its profoundest. The principle is to grant to every thought or character or aspect of existence full and equal rights and perfect liberty to develop and flower. Just as no perception or issue is too trivial (trivial by conventional standards) for Proust to write ten or a hundred pages about it, so no judgement is passed on Proust's characters by his method of description. He abjures all traditional frameworks or conventions, like satire or pathos or burlesque, which might direct the reader's response. If a character is a fool or a knave, he or she will have to prove it, and the reader is given all the evidence, not just a slanted selection, on which to form a judgement. Hence it is only imperceptibly that the reader comes to realize that M. de Norpois is a monstrous old bully and windbag; and it is always up to the reader, nor does Proust in any way prohibit it, to come to quite another conclusion and find M. de Norpois a delightful and worldly-wise figure 'of the old school'.

Now the tendency of this method of Proust's is profoundly egalitarian. People sometimes refer to Proust as a 'snob', meaning a title-hunter, but they tend to confuse three different things. Marcel was undoubtedly a title-hunter, Proust may have been one, but his book, surely, is peculiarly unsnobbish. That it can devote two hundred pages to a party at the princesse de Parme's shows just how much it has freed itself from social absolutes and is able to study 'the purely social' with a free and adventurous intellect. Nor need we react with cynicism when Marcel declares he is totally devoid of 'class' feelings. ('I had never made distinctions between classes.') For if I say that Marcel is a title-lover, I do not mean that he is a full-time or quintessential one; it is only one of his many adolescent idealizations, like his idealization of Venice or of the *jeunes filles*.

Marcel's declaration is indeed of great interst, and no doubt it is not far from Proust's own view of himself. The liftboy at the Balbec hotel has told Marcel that someone has called on him in his absence; and when Marcel asks who it was, he replies: 'It was the *monsieur* you went out with yesterday.' Marcel takes this to mean Saint-Loup. It turns out, however, that the liftboy was referring to Marcel's chauffeur; and Marcel is struck by this lesson, that a working-man, as well as a man of fashion, may be a '*monsieur*'.

A lesson in words only. For as regards the *thing* I had never made distinctions between classes. And if, hearing a chauffeur referred to as a *monsieur*, I had the same surprise as Count X, who had only been a Count for eight days and whom, by saying to him 'The Countess looks tired', I had caused to look round to see whom I was talking about, it was simply a matter of not being used to the vocabulary; I had never made any distinction between workers, *bourgeois* and *grands seigneurs*, and I would have chosen one or other as friends with equal ease. With a certain preference for workers, and after that for *grands seigneurs*, not as a matter of taste, but knowing that you could expect more politeness towards workers from them than you could from *bourgeois*, whether because *grands seigneurs* do not despise workers as *bourgeois* do, or because they are polite on principle to anyone, no matter whom, like pretty women who are happy to bestow a smile when they know that it will be received with such joy.[14]

If Proust's work is, in its very method, egalitarian, so even more plainly is Joyce's. The subject Joyce set himself in *Ulysses* was clearly chosen as a deliberate challenge to the 'modernist' method. There could be no hero more vulnerable to Edwardian social prejudice than Bloom—not only a Jew, but a commercial traveller, which in genteel mythology was a kind of archetype of vulgarity. That the method was triumphant, and Bloom's grandeur established, most of us would agree. Joyce gives the most precise and delicate registration of the social pinpricks and blows that Bloom suffers throughout the day—for instance the undercurrent of snubbing that runs through the Hades scene, culminating in John Henry Menton's blank stare when Bloom tells him his hat is dented. Nevertheless the effect is altogether different from what it would have been in Thackeray or Meredith, or for that matter in Arnold Bennett or H. G. Wells. These things seem, with Joyce, to be offered for our dispassionate contemplation, enabling us to see through and also *round* them; and the reason, or one of the reasons, is that no social relationship has been set up between the author and the reader. The category of 'the social' is given no special and privileged fictional status and goes down in the general bonfire of categories.

In this connection the career of Ford Madox Ford is illuminating. Few novelists have been so obsessed and ensnared by social absolutes. Ezra Pound's friendly home truth seems to have been plumb right: 'Fordie, you 'AVE got a rummy lot of "*idées reçues*". Not sure the beastly word gentleman hasn't caused you more trouble in your bright li'l life than all the rest of the lang.'[15] In his Tietjens tetralogy Ford, through some deep artistic miscalculation, seems to be asking us to endorse Tietjens's own English-country-gentleman attitudes, some of which—in Ford's version of them—are entirely preposterous. (Among novels of the same degree of seriousness, *Parade's End* must take the prize for weird *dicta*. What is one to do with such a remark as Tietjens's about his eldest brother: 'He has got a French woman near Euston station. He's lived with her for over fifteen years, of afternoons, when there were no race meetings'? It is a remark that belongs only on the revue stage.)

How Ford escaped from this *impasse* in his one undoubted masterpiece, *The Good Soldier*, is that he here adopted a certain 'French' stance, learned from his friends Conrad and Henry James. For those foreign and Frenchifying novelists a favourite subject-matter was, very properly, Englishness—English 'honour', English manners, English inarticulacy—which they liked to present to themselves as a great mystery. Now Ford, though he had a German father, was as English as could be; nevertheless for the purposes of this one novel he was able to think himself into a foreigner's detachment. His mode of telling the story, through the eyes of an alien (the American innocent, Dowell) allowed him to make 'English-gentlemanliness' the heart of his novel, not as an 'absolute' but as an exotic enigma and case to be studied.

It is an obvious point, yet one worth making, that the device of 'interior monologue' militates against social absolutes and works strongly in favour of egalitarianism, indeed almost compels it. I am not meaning to imply a simple-minded view of 'interior monologue', which is as arbitrary a literary convention as any other, though so wonderfully fruitful in Joyce's hands. Still, it must be granted to it that, in theory anyway, it throws down social barriers: it bypasses or overleaps the problem of the author's social relationship to his or her characters. Social rules and prejudices express themselves in terms of distance, and 'interior monologue' asserts a total intimacy which must preclude 'distance'.

One sometimes feels it a pity that Virginia Woolf did not trust interior monologue more. Every now and then her novels seem to run aground on the rock of social prejudice, in a way from which this technique might actually have preserved her. I am thinking of her portrait of Miss Kilman in *Mrs Dalloway*, the dowdy and unhappy spinster who tutors Mrs Dalloway's daughter in history. Miss Kilman is hated by Mrs Dalloway, in whose eyes she appears as ugly, self-righteous, envious, and a bad influence on her daughter; and she fares no better in direct description by Virginia Woolf, nor does Woolf trouble always to make it clear whose account we are reading, hers or Mrs Dalloway's. Then, in the painful scene in which Miss Kilman alienates even the Dalloway daughter, whom she idolizes, we are taken half inside Miss Kilman's consciousness—but only half inside, for Woolf uses the third-person method, and we still feel the presence of the author, exaggerating, caricaturing and passing social judgement.

But to sit here, unable to think of anything to say; to see Elizabeth turning against her; to be felt repulsive even by her—it was too much; she could not stand it. The thick fingers curled inwards.

'I never go to parties,' said Miss Kilman, just to keep Elizabeth from going. 'People don't ask me to parties'—and she knew as she said it that it was this egotism that was her undoing; Mr Whittaker had warned her; but she could not help it. She had suffered so horribly. 'Why should they ask me?' she said. 'I'm plain, I'm unhappy.' She knew it was idiotic. But it was all those people passing—people with parcels who despised her—who made her say it. However, she was Doris Kilman. She had her degree. She was a woman who had made her way in the world. Her knowledge of modern history was more than respectable.[16]

The effect of this passage for the reader is of a great unfairness, amounting to gratuitous cruelty. Of course, it is not just a question of technique, and no doubt if Tolstoy had used the same technique we would have felt no such moral objection. Nevertheless, if Virginia Woolf had committed herself here to true 'interior monologue' she would, almost of necessity, also have found herself committed to more fellow-feeling.

Humanism as introspection

A very elementary, yet nevertheless important, point about the history of the novel is that novelists have steadily grown more intimate with their characters. We are more in the intimacy of Jane Austen's Emma than we are of the characters of Fielding or Fanny Burney and more in the intimacy of Maggie Tulliver than in that of Emma, and these are as nothing compared to the intimacies risked by Tolstoy and James Joyce. Now it is above all to intimacy that imagined 'class-distinctions' are a barrier. 'Class' is a barrier phenomenon, a concept only experienced vividly by people when in the presence of a barrier. It prompts nausea or yearning: a nausea at the idea of personal closeness, and a turning-of-the-back on a whole imagined 'class'; or a yearning for personal closeness, leading to the romanticizing of a whole imagined 'class'. Thus it follows that 'class' is likely to be a clog to the progress of fiction.

According to Hannah Arendt, intimacy is a comparatively recent invention. Its first explorer and theorist, she asserts, was Jean-Jacques Rousseau ('the only great author still frequently cited by his first name alone'), and it developed side-by-side with, and in opposition to, another new arrival, the 'social'—this opposition effectively replacing the older classical one of the 'public' versus the 'private'. The result, she says, was 'the astonishing flowering' of poetry and music (the 'intimate' arts) from the mid-eighteenth century until almost the last third of the nineteenth and the simultaneous rise of the novel, 'the only entirely social art form'—a process accompanied by 'a no less striking decline of all the public arts, especially architecture'.[17]

It is a suggestive theory, from which we may take the point that the novel, if it is the 'only entirely social art form', is likely to have a problem in regard to its enemy the 'intimate'. Well, as we know, it did have such a problem; and the remedy to which, increasingly, it resorted was 'impersonality'—a doctrine of cardinal importance to Flaubert and to Joyce.

We need to be careful not to misunderstand this. It would, for one thing, be a mistake (a mistake sometimes made by their imitators) to confuse 'impersonality', as they practised it, with 'distance' in the social sense; these writers are not putting their characters in their place, like some seventeenth-century grandee. Their attitude, indeed, seems much more a kind of indirect or inverted fellow-feeling. Sartre, in *L'Idiot de la famille*, argues that what Flaubert and his fellow *chevaliers du néant* ('knights of nihilism') were doing, in their stance of impassivity or cruel detachment, was to interiorize the stony quality of capitalist property-relationships; but against this there is an obstinate objection, that what we feel in reading *Madame Bovary* and *L'Éducation sentimentale* is an extreme poignancy, and a powerful impression of fellow-feeling.

Something similar may be said of Michel Foucault's explanation of 'impersonality' in terms of 'the death of the author'.[18] It is true, as Foucault says, that 'modernist' writing involved, typically, a sacrifice of the life to the work. 'The work, which once had the duty of providing immortality, now possesses the right to kill, to be its author's murderer, as in the case of Flaubert, Proust, and Kafka.' We can agree, too, with his account of 'impersonality' as a matter of the writer 'assuming the role of the dead man in the game of writing'. What seems wrong is the leap made by Foucault to the 'death of man'—which, according to Nietzsche, is implied in the 'death of God'. One has only to think of Kafka, who, if he 'assumes the role of the dead man in the game of writing', does so, surely for no anti-humanist motives? Indeed, if his work can be said to have a leading theme, it seems to be an extreme horror of de-humanization? There is no mistaking the meaning of that last sentence in *Metamorphosis*, in which we read how Gregor's sister, at the end of the tram-journey with her parents, and as confirmation of their 'new dreams and excellent intentions' about finding her a husband, 'sprang to her feet first and stretched her young body'. It is she, not Gregor, who is being envisaged as a beetle. The unforgettable final paragraph of 'A Hunger Artist' works to rather similar effect; indeed you might almost think of it as a deliberate counterblast to Nietzsche.

'Well, clear this out now!' said the overseer, and they buried the hunger artist, straw and all. Into the cage they put a young panther. Even the most insensitive felt it refreshing to see this wild creature leaping around the cage that had so long been dreary. The panther was all right. The food he liked was brought to him without hesitation by the attendants; he seemed not even to miss his freedom; his noble body, furnished almost to the bursting point with all that it needed, seemed to carry freedom around with it too; it seemed to lurk somewhere in his jaws . . .

What strikes one, indeed, is that the work of Kafka, Proust and Joyce seems dedicated, not just in its outlook but in its very techniques, to the value of the human and to human solidarity. It is a technical innovation in Kafka that the reader is instantly and deeply drawn in to some human dilemma or 'case' but does not know in the least where he, as reader, belongs. His relationship to the human circumstances, far from stony detachment, is a sense of being jostled from pillar to post—of not knowing, as you might say, which part of speech in the sentence (subject? object? verb?) he or she represents. Whichever attitude he chooses to espouse, it will lead him where he never intended to go and into the awkwardest ethical corners. The effect is not just egalitarian (the reader being thus stripped of privileges) but insistently directed towards human solidarity.

It is worth remembering that Conrad, in his aesthetic manifesto, the Preface to *The Nigger of the 'Narcissus'*, explicitly links solidarity to introspection. The artist's response to the visible universe, he says, is different from the 'thinker's' or the 'scientist's'. 'Impressed by the aspect of the world the thinker plunges into ideas, the scientist into facts . . . It is otherwise with the artist. Confronted by the same enigmatical spectacle the artist descends within himself, and in that lonely region of stress and strife, if he be deserving and fortunate, he finds the terms of his appeal.' And the reason for this, says Conrad, is that the appeal of art is to human solidarity, 'to the subtle but invincible conviction of solidarity that knits together the loneliness of innumerable hearts . . .'.

I really believe there is a truth to be discovered about 'the nature of the novel' and that the later nineteenth-century novelists, Conrad among them, got nearer to understanding it than their predecessors—and that it is a truth with implications beyond the novel. The truth concerns the personal, or perhaps I should say the grammatical, relationship of the novelist to his or her creation. It is the truth enshrined in those commonplaces of literary history, that Madame Bovary *is* Flaubert, that George Eliot found Mr Casaubon in her own breast and her own self-doubts,* that Joyce is both Stephen Dedalus and Bloom. It is the truth that a novel has to be produced by introspection and impersonation and that what we are confronted with is not so much Lord Jim as Conrad-as-Lord-Jim.† Proust stated the other side of the same truth when he wrote that it is only out of habit, 'a habit contracted from the insincere language of prefaces and dedications', that the writer speaks of 'my reader'.

In reality every reader is, while he is reading, the reader of his own self. The writer's work is merely a kind of optical instrument which he offers to the reader to enable him to discern what, without this book, he would perhaps never have perceived in himself.[19]

What prevents the truth from being quite obvious seems to be a fundamental and atavistic misconception of what a novel is. Somewhere in the back of readers' and critics' minds there lurks, unexamined, the idea that a novel is 'like' life. Long ago, no doubt, they will have thrown away the vulgarer versions of this idea: for instance, that novels 'reflect' life, or can be mirror-like or camera-like, or that there is some quasi-mechanical fashion in which human life can be recorded. For all that, the idea of likeness infects their way of regarding the novel. This is curious, if one considers it. It would never occur to anyone to say of a poem that it is like, or unlike, the things it deals with; nor does it really help to do so with a novel. Indeed the only reason why it was ever thought to seems to be that, by an old and vapid convention, novels have tended to be talked about in terms of 'painting' and the plastic arts. Evidently a painting (at all events a representational painting) is, in a crude but important sense, *like* life. A painting (and much more so a sculpture) could conceivably actually be mistaken for the thing it represents; whereas no one ever mistook a bound copy of *Jane Eyre* for Jane, Mr Rochester,

---

* When a young admirer asked George Eliot, 'But from whom, then, did you draw Casaubon?' the novelist, 'with a humorous solemnity which was quite in earnest, nevertheless, pointed to her own heart'. (See G. S. Haight, *George Eliot: a Biography* (1968), p.450.)

† One thinks of *A Passage to India* in which, in Mrs Moore, Forster represents his imaginary best self and deepest fears, in Ralph Moore provides a vividly realized version of his younger self, and in Adela Quested is re-enacting a childhood trauma, the episode of 'the man in the deerstalker hat'. (See my *E. M. Forster: a Life*, vol. 1 (1977), p. 38.)

or Lowood School. The relationships between a novel and 'life' are fundamentally not different from those between a poem and 'life'. They offer the spectacle of every kind of transformation, transposition, metonymy, synecdoche, Yeatsian antithesis and the like; and the utter unlikeness to 'life' of the medium—whether we define the medium as a bound book with numbered pages, or as a sequence of sentences, or as a participation in events which it is magically open to the reader at any instant to arrest—will also be crucial to the novel's existence.

Proust's formulation, that 'in reality every reader is, while he is reading, the reader of his own self', is a declaration of human solidarity. For to create by self-scrutiny almost by definition abolishes social barriers: one cannot hold a part of oneself at a social distance. It is also, fairly plainly, an assertion of belief in a 'human nature', though a very flexible human nature. Thus he writes:

The writer must not be indignant if the invert who reads his book gives to his heroines a masculine countenance. For only by the indulgence of this slightly aberrant peculiarity can the invert give to what he is reading its full general import . . . if M. de Charlus had not bestowed upon the 'traîtresse' for whom Musset weeps in *La Nuit d'Octobre* or *Le Souvenir* the features of Morel, he would neither have wept nor have understood.[20]

What is further implied in Proust's theory, however, is rejection of the notion of the novelist as privileged to exclude himself from his novel, and as standing towards his characters in some 'Cartesian' relationship of observer to observed, in favour of a more 'Heideggerian' conception, best expressed by the question, 'What do we mean by "looking at ourself"?' It makes sense to speak of 'looking at ourself', but the more one puzzles over it (and whether one is thinking of the body or of the mind and personality) the more complicated a notion it seems. The problems attending looking at one's face (it comes out reversed) or looking at one's body (one can only see certain portions of it) have their parallels in looking at oneself as a character; and it is with similar problems, according to Proust, that the novel is concerned. According to this view, each human being comprises, potentially, the characteristics of the whole human race; and the novel's great feat is to enable him to perceive more of these characteristics but by methods far removed from stock notions: 'observation', 'description', 'likeness-to-life' etc.

The bearing of all this on 'class', the 'gentleman' and such-like social absolutes, is, I hope, clear. It would seem that the 'modernist' novelists, by their very methods and innovations, offered a principled defiance to such absolutes. The assumption on which 'honour'-systems are based is that there are, in theory at least, some people (a 'rabble') without honour ('We must exclude someone from our gathering, or we shall be left with nothing'). It was, by contrast, a point of pride with 'modernist' novels to exclude nobody, and no topic, and to admit no barriers—thus Robert Musil organized his novel round the two quite remote consciousnesses of Ulrich, the 'Man Without Qualities', and of Moosbrugger, the condemned carpenter and sex-criminal, on the assumption that the two would gravitate together according to some quite general law (' . . . somehow Ulrich could not help thinking: if mankind could dream collectively, it would dream Moosbrugger'[21]).

Equally, the guilty secret of 'class' is that one can pretend to have opted out from the system of 'class' and be speaking from some privileged standpoint outside it—whilst all the time vigorously exploiting it; and the 'modernist' novels were, in their most basic procedures, designed to repudiate the self-exclusion or 'opting-out' fallacy. Thackeray perceived the issue but could only envisage it in the form of a trap: that to be concerned with 'snobbery' is itself snobbish, so that there is an infinite regress and no escape. Flaubert also perceived it, for this is what governs his attitude to the bourgeois—that it was for him a matter of *self*-scrutiny and *self*-mortification. But he acknowledged it in chagrin and with a sigh. By contrast the 'modernist' novels, which raised the issue as an epistemological and universally human one, were able to give it a more liberating and optimistic answer. If there is an escape from 'class', it must come, not by ignoring it, but by thinking it through, as a prelude to *un*-thinking it; and in this project it could be said that, up to now, these novels have been our most hopeful guide.

NOTES AND REFERENCES

PART 1

THE MEANING OF 'CLASS'

1 The rhetoric of 'class'

1 From J. Betjeman, 'Beside the Seaside', in *Collected Poems*, (1978) p. 163.
2 See A. Marwick, *Class: Image and Reality* (1980), *passim*.
3 L. Wittgenstein, *Philosophical Investigations*, trans. G. E. M. Anscombe (3rd edn., 1968), p. 20.
4 In *Essays in Labour History*, ed. Asa Briggs and J. Saville (1960).
5 e.g. William Wilberforce's *Practical View of the Prevailing Religious Systems of Professed Christians in the Higher and Middle Classes of this Country Contrasted with Real Christianity* (1797).
6 G. Duby, *Les Trois Ordres: ou l'imaginaire du féodalisme* (1978).
7 G. Dumézil, *Mythe et épopée* (1968), p. 16.
8 *Monthly Repository* (1834), p. 320; quoted by Raymond Williams in *Keywords* (1976), p. 58.
9 Speech in the House of Lords, 7 Oct. 1831 in *Speeches of Henry Lord Brougham* (1838), vol. 2, pp. 600–1.
10 K. Clark, *The Making of Victorian England* (1962), pp. 5–6.
11 D. Defoe, *Robinson Crusoe* (1719), chapter 1.
12 Mary Wollstonecraft, *Vindication of the Rights of Women* (1792), p. 5.
13 J. Mill, *Government* (1821), p. 31.
14 See J. Morley, *Life of Richard Cobden* (1879), vol. 1, p. 249.
15 There is an excellent article on it by Asa Briggs, 'Middle-class consciousness in English politics 1780–1846', in *Past and Present*, no. 9 (1956), pp. 65–74.
16 D. Davie, *These the Companions* (1982), p. 2.
17 Ibid. 3.
18 M. Arnold, *Culture and Anarchy* (1869), p. 95.
19 E. B. Lytton, *England and the English* (1833), p. 32.
20 So it would appear from a quotation from Lytton in Michael Sadleir's *Bulwer: A Panorama* (1931), p. 324; but, oddly, I cannot trace the edition Sadleir is quoting from.
21 'The hon. Gentleman, and other hon. Gentlemen, are pleased to designate me as the arch enemy of farmers. Sir, I have as good a right as any hon. Gentleman in this House to identify myself with the order of farmers. I am a farmer's son . . . my ancestors were all yeomen of the class who have been suffering under this system.'
22 Quoted by John Morley in *The Life of Richard Cobden* (1879), vol. 1, p. 269.
23 Speech to the Council of the League, Manchester, Sept. 1842 (ibid. 249).
24 Quoted in Morley, ibid. vol. 1, pp. 390–7.
25 Marx, *Contribution to a Critique of Hegel's Philosophy of Law: Introduction*, in *Collected Works*, vol. 3 (1975), p. 186.
26 See p. 12.

27 C. Lucas, 'Nobles, Bourgeois and the French Revolution', in *French Society and the Revolution*, ed. D. Johnson (1976), p. 99.
28 Ibid. 103.
29 F. Engels, *The Condition of the Working Class in England*, trans. W. O. Henderson and W. H. Chaloner (1971), p. 311.

2 'The bourgeoisie'

1 See P. Calvert, *The Concept of Class* (1982), pp. 18–25 and Dallas L. Clouatre, 'The Concept of Class in French Culture Prior to the Revolution', *Journal of the History of Ideas*, April–June 1984, 14, no. 2, pp. 233–44.
2 W. H. Sewell, Jr., *Work and Revolution in France: The Language of Labor from the Old Regime to 1848*, p. 283.
3 See Shirley Gruner, 'The Revolution of July 1830 and the expression "Bourgeoisie" ', *The Historical Journal*,' 11, 3 (1968), pp. 462–71.
4 See E. Huguet, *Dictionnaire de la langue française du 16me siècle* (1932).
5 See Norbert Elias, *The Civilising Process: The History of Manners*, trans. E. Jephcott (1978), pp. 109–11. (First published 1939 as *Über den Prozess der Zivilisation*.)
6 Lucas, op. cit. 94.
7 *Papiers inédits trouvés chez Ropespierre* [*sic*], *Saint-Just, Paysan* etc., vol. 2 (1828), p. 15.
8 The armed rising on 2 June in Paris, which led to the purge of Girondins from the Convention.
9 Speech to the Convention, 31 Aug. 1893; in *Discours de Danton*, ed. A. Fribourg (1910), p. 508.
10 Quoted in *French Revolution Documents*, vol. 2, ed. J. M. Roberts and J. Hardman (1973), p. 243.
11 M. Proust, *Le Côté de Guermantes*, (Pléiade edn), vol. 2, p. 455.
12 I am here following Shirley Gruner's account, already cited; see note 3 above.
13 *The Reminiscences of Karl Schurz* (1909), vol. 1, p. 138; quoted by David McLellan in *Karl Marx: His Life and Thought* (1973), p. 453.
14 Quoted by McLellan, ibid., p. 313.
15 Flaubert, *Correspondance* (Pléiade edn), vol. 1, p. 630.
16 Ibid. 268.
17 Letter to Louise Colet, 29 Aug. 1847.
18 The remark is quoted by Lionel Trilling in *Beyond Culture* (Uniform edn, 1980), p. 26.
19 W. H. Auden, 'Authority in America', *The Griffin*, 1955.
20 Jean-Paul Sartre, *L'Idiot de la famille*, vol. 3 (1972), p. 454.
21 Ibid. 208.

3 Marx's unwritten chapter

1 Karl Marx, *Capital*, vol. 3, chapter 52.
2 Marx, 'Zirkularbrief' to Bebel and others (1879), in *Critique of the Gotha Programme* (new edn, Berlin, 1946) p. 102.
3 *Capital*, vol. 3, chapter 52.

4 Marx, *The Eighteenth Brumaire of Louis Bonaparte*, in *Collected Works*, vol. 11 (1979), p. 128.

5 Marx, *Communist Manifesto*, in *Collected Works*, vol. 6 (1976), *passim*.

6 Ibid. 482.

7 Marx, *The Poverty of Philosophy*, in *Collected Works*, vol. 6 (1976), p. 212.

8 Marx, *German Ideology*, in *Collected Works*, vol. 5 (1976), p. 77.

9 Marx, *The Holy Family*, in *Collected Works*, vol. 4 (1975), p. 37.

10 *The Eighteenth Brumaire*, p. 187.

11 *The Poverty of Philosophy*, p. 211.

12 Marx and Engels, *The Communist Manifesto* (Centenary edn, 1948) pp. 15–16.

13 Ibid. 16.

14 'Tories and Whigs', *New York Daily Tribune* 21 Aug. 1852; in *Surveys from Exile*, ed. D. Fernback (1973), p. 257.

15 Sometimes translated as 'Philosophy of Right' (see next note).

16 *Hegel's Philosophy of Right*, trans. T. M. Knox (1965), pp. 153–4. Knox's misleading rendering, however, is 'cannot live in the manner of his *class*'.

17 See O. Ladendorf, *Historisches Schlagwörterbuch* (1906), s.v. *Proletarier*.

18 Marx, *Critique of Hegel's Philosophy of Right*, ed. J. O'Malley (1970). The extracts from Hegel in O'Malley's edition are taken from T. M. Knox's translation, where *Stand* again tends to be translated as 'class'.

19 *Contribution to a Critique . . . Introduction*, p. 184.

20 Quoted by David Shub in *Lenin: A Biography* (Penguin edn, 1966), p. 366.

4   'Class' and the historians

1 A. Cobban, 'The Vocabulary of Social History', *Political Science Quarterly*, 71, no. 1 (1956), p. 5.

2 Gruner, loc. cit. 471.

3 A. Jouanna, *Ordre social: mythes et hiérarchies dans la France du XVIe siècle* (1977), p. 7.

4 See Everitt and Stone, conference papers on 'Social Mobility in England', *Past and Present*, no. 33, April 1966, pp. 72, 53–4.

5 E. P. Thompson, 'Eighteenth-century English society: class-struggle without class?', *Social History*, 3, no. 2, May 1978, pp. 133–65.

6 Ibid. 145.

7 See R. S. Neale, 'Class and Class-consciousness in early nineteenth-century England: Three classes or five?', *Victorian Studies*, 12, (1968–9), p. 23.

8 First published 1969; English translation by Steve Cox 1973.

9 'The entire shopkeeper group can be left among the "médiocres", where they were assigned in the previous chapter' (p. 244).

10 J. H. Hexter, *Reappraisals in History* (1961), p. 74.

5   'Class' and the sociologists

1 R. Dahrendorf, *Class and Class Conflict in Industrial Society* (1959), p. 74.

2 Ibid. 75.

3 W. G. Runciman, *Social Science and Political Theory* (2nd edn, 1969), p. 139.

4 Ibid 136.

5 Dahrendorf, op. cit. 75.

6 R. Bendix and S. Lipset, eds, *Class, Status and Power* (1954), p. 77.

7 Ibid. 87–92.
8 Ibid. 81–2.
9 Ibid. 89.
10 Ibid. 69.
11 W. B. Gallie, 'Essentially contested concepts', *Proceedings of the Aristotelian Society*, New Series, 56 (1956), p. 169.
12 Bendix and Lipset, op. cit. 88.
13 R. Mousnier, *Les Hiérarchies sociales de 1450 à nos jours* (1969), pp. 11–15.

PART 2

BEFORE 'CLASS', AND AFTER

6 The 'social hierarchy'

1 A. de Tocqueville, *Democracy in America*, trans. G. Lawrence (Fontana edn, 1968) vol. 2, p. 653.
2 P. Zagorin, *The Court and the Country* (1969), p. 23.
3 See *Memoirs of the Duc de Saint-Simon*, ed. and trans. W. H. Lewis (1964), pp. 27–8.
4 P. Zagorin, op. cit. 25.
5 Sylvia Thrupp, *The Merchant Class of Medieval London* (1948), p. 299.
6 S. Johnson, Review of Soame Jenyns's *A Free Inquiry into the Nature and Origin of Evil*; *Literary Magazine* (1757), p. 372
7 R. Gough, *The History of Myddle*, ed. D. Hey (Penguin edn, 1981).
8 Ibid. 78.
9 Ibid. 119.
10 Ibid. 78.
11 L. Stone, 'Social Mobility in England, 1500 to 1700', *Past and Present* no. 33, April 1966, pp. 16–55.
12 See P. Laslett, *The World We Have Lost—further explored* (1965), p. 38.
13 Quoted by Michel Foucault in *Les Mots et les choses* (1955), p. 7.

7 Honour and the *honnête*

1 See Calvert, op. cit. 173.
2 Lewis, op. cit. 51.
3 See Thrupp, op. cit. 259–60.
4 See May McKisack, *The Fourteenth Century 1307–1399* (1959), p. 143.
5 M. Proust, *Le Côté de Guermantes* (Pléiade edn), vol. 2, p. 35.
6 *Honour and Shame: The Values of Mediterranean Society*, ed. J. G. Peristiany (1965), p. 15.
7 J. A. Sharpe, *Defamation and Sexual Slander in Early Modern England: The Church Courts at York* (Borthwick Institute of Historical Research, Borthwick Papers No. 58 (1980)).
8 M. Girouard, *Life in the English Country House* (Penguin edn, 1980), p. 85.
9 Yves Castan, *Honnêteté et relations sociales en Languedoc 1715–1780* (1974), p. 179.
10 G. Eliot, *The Mill on the Floss* (1860), Book 1, chapter 6.
11 Ibid.
12 See Domna C. Stanton, *The Aristocrat as Art* (1980).
13 Castan, op. cit. 21–2.

14 Andreas Capellanus, *The Art of Courtly Love*, trans. John J. Parry (1941): quoted in *The History of Feudalism*, ed. D. Herlihy (1970), p. 55.
15 Chesterfield, *Letters to his Son*: 14 Nov. 1749.
16 Ibid.: 28 Feb. 1751.

8 The 'gentleman'

1 See K. B. McFarlane, *The English Nobility, 1290–1536* (1973), pp. 122–5.
2 See Thrupp, op. cit. 236.
3 K. B. McFarlane, *The Nobility of Later Medieval England* (1973), p. 275.
4 T. Smith, *De republica Anglorum* (1583), pp. 31–2.
5 G. D. Squibb, *The High Court of Chivalry* (1959), p. 173.
6 Defoe, *Robinson Crusoe*, Chapter 1.
7 See W. Empson, *The Structure of Complex Words* (1951), chapters 9–11, *passim*.
8 *Guardian*, no. 34 (20 April 1713).
9 R. Gilmour, *The Idea of the Gentleman in the Victorian Novel* (1981), pp. 10–11.
10 W. Empson, 'Tom Jones', *Kenyon Review*, 20, 1958.
11 H. Fielding, *Tom Jones*, Book 9, chapter 7.
12 Gilmour, op. cit. 2.
13 G. Eliot, *Felix Holt the Radical* (1866), chapter 2.
14 Ibid. chapter 5.
15 W. Bagehot, *The English Constitution*, in *Collected Works*, ed. N. St John-Stevas, vol. 5 (1974), p. 378.
16 See J. Milroy, 'On the sociolinguistic history of /h/-dropping in English', in *Current Topics in English Historical Linguistics*, ed. M. Davenport *et al.* (Odense University Studies in English, 4, 1981).
17 I cannot find h-dropping discussed in Samuel Pegge's exhaustive *Anecdotes of the English Language, Chiefly Regarding the Local Dialect of London* (1803).
18 H. Alford, *The Queen's English* (3rd edn, 1870), p. 51.
19 Gilmour, op. cit. 70.
20 A. Trollope, *Autobiography* (1883), p. 53.
21 Gilmour, op. cit. 109.

9 Nietzsche revised

1 Nietzsche, *The Genealogy of Morals*, trans. H. B. Samuel (1910), pp. 19–20
2 Ibid. 34–5.
3 E. Le Roy Ladurie, *Montaillou* (Penguin edn, 1980), p. 57.
4 Quoted by Brian Manning in *The English People and the English Revolution* (1976), p. 318 (italics mine).
5 *Life of Robert Owen by Himself* (1920 edn) pp. 122–3; quoted by Harold Perkin, *The Origins of Modern English Society 1780–1880* (1969), p. 279.
6 M. Proust, *A l'ombre des jeunes filles en fleurs*, (Pléiade edn), vol. 1, p. 758.
7 Thrupp, op. cit. 16.
8 Castan, op. cit. 23.
9 Bagehot, op. cit. 311.
10 Peristiany, op. cit. 38.
11 Ibid. 37.
12 L. Dumont, *Homo Hierarchicus* (1967), p. 67.
13 N. Mitford and A. Ross, *Noblesse Oblige* (1956), pp. 78–9.

14 Ibid. 74.
15 Quoted by Brian Manning in 'The Aristocracy and the Downfall of Charles I', in *Politics, Religion and the English Civil War*, ed. B. Manning (1973), p. 40.
16 See Mark Girouard, 'Parades and Promenades', *Listener*, 13 Oct. 1983, pp. 16–18.
17 P. Brendon, *Head of Guinness* (privately printed, 1979), p. 148.
18 Quoted in Girouard, *Life in the English Country House*, p. 285.
19 Quoted in Perkin, op. cit. 202.
20 Elias, op. cit. 206–10.
21 Ibid. 209.
22 Castan, see above, pp. 88–9.
23 See J. P. Sartre, *L'Être et le néant* (1943), Part III, chapter 3, section 3.
24 Ibid. 470.
25 D. H. Lawrence, *Sons and Lovers* (1913), chapter 10.
26 D. H. Lawrence, 'Autobiographical Sketch', *Phoenix II* (1968), p. 595. (I have borrowed these two examples from an essay 'D. H. Lawrence and Class' by Graham Martin, in *The Uses of Fiction: Essays on the Modern Novel in Honour of Arnold Kettle*, ed. D. Jefferson and G. Martin (1982), pp. 83–97).
27 Calvert, op. cit. 216.

10   The escape

1 L. Trilling, *The Liberal Imagination* (1956), pp. 205–22.
2 Ibid. 211.
3 Ibid.
4 Ibid. 211–12.
5 W. M. Thackeray, *The Newcomes* (1853), chapter 7.
6 A. Trollope, *Can You Forgive Her?* (1864), chapter 17.
7 J. Cary, 'The Tough World of Surtees', *Sunday Times*, 14 April 1957.
8 'Mr Jorrocks at Margate'.
9 See the speech by Brougham quoted on p. 9.
10 G. K. Chesterton, 'Dombey and Son', in *Criticisms and Appreciations of The Works of Charles Dickens* (1911), p. 125.
11 C. Dickens, *Nicholas Nickleby*, (1838) chapter 16.
12 C. Dickens, *The Old Curiosity Shop* (1841), chapter 26.
13 E. B. Lytton, *England and the English* (1833) vol. 1, p. 29.
14 M. Proust, *Sodome et Gomorrhe* (Pléiade edn), vol. 2, pp. 1026–7.
15 Ezra Pound to Ford Madox Ford, 27 Dec. 1933; quoted in Frank MacShane, *The Life and Works of Ford Madox Ford* (1965), p. 232.
16 V. Woolf, *Mrs Dalloway* (Uniform edn, 1929), pp. 199–200.
17 H. Arendt, *The Human Condition* (1958), p. 39.
18 M. Foucault, 'What Is an Author?', trans. J. V. Harari, in *Textual Strategies*, ed. J. V. Harari (1979), pp. 141–60.
19 M. Proust, *Le Temps retrouvé* (Pléiade edn.), vol. 3, p. 911.
20 Proust, loc. cit.
21 R. Musil, *The Man Without Qualities*, trans. E. Wilkins and E. Kaiser (Picador edn, 1979), vol. 1, p. 85.

INDEX